ALSO BY BRUCE D. BERKOWITZ

*American Security: Dilemmas
for a Modern Democracy*

CALCULATED
RISKS
A Century of
Arms Control, Why It Has Failed,
and How It Can Be Made to Work

Bruce D. Berkowitz

SIMON AND SCHUSTER
New York

Published by Simon and Schuster
A Division of Simon & Schuster, Inc.
Simon & Schuster Building
Rockefeller Center
1230 Avenue of the Americas
New York, NY 10020
SIMON AND SCHUSTER is a registered trademark of
Simon & Schuster, Inc.

Designed by Irving Perkins Associates

Manufactured in the United States of America

1   2   3   4   5   6   7   8   9   10

Library of Congress Cataloging in Publication Data
Berkowitz, Bruce D.
Calculated risks.

Bibliography: p.
Includes index.
1. Arms control—History.   2. Nuclear arms control—
United States—History.   3. Nuclear arms control—
Soviet Union—History.   I. Title.
JX1974.B426   1987   327.1'74'09   87–9763

ISBN 0–671–60087–7

ACKNOWLEDGMENTS

Throughout the writing of this book, I have benefited from the comments of many individuals who were kind enough to share their knowledge and experience. In particular, I am pleased to thank Richard K. Betts, Bruce Bueno de Mesquita, Alton Frye, Bernard F. McMahon, Lori Murray, David Rosenberg, Henry S. Rowen, Thomas Powers, Paul Stares, and James Tritten. The writing of this book was supported by a Guest Scholarship at the Brookings Institution; special thanks are due to Bruce K. MacLaury, President of Brookings, and John D. Steinbruner, director of the Foreign Policy Studies Program there.

As former intelligence analysts remain under certain voluntarily accepted obligations, I appreciated the expeditious review of the manuscript by the Publications Review Board at the Central Intelligence Agency (though, of course, the material and analysis contained here are my own and do not necessarily reflect the views of the Central Intelligence Agency, the Brookings Institution, or any other organization).

This book originated from a series of conversations I had with Robert Asahina, editor at Simon and Schuster; it can truly be said the book would not have happened were it not for his efforts, and much of the final product bears his mark.

Several people provided much-needed moral support at critical points during the writing of the manuscript, and so I offer many thanks to Rich and Cyndy, Carol, and, most especially, the gracious lady to whom this book is dedicated.

5

To
Mary Alice

CONTENTS

CONTENTS

CHAPTER ONE

Introduction

FEW subjects in foreign policy receive as much attention today as arms control. It is difficult to imagine any major national politician without a clear stand on the desirability of arms control, and probably no other foreign policy issue has so captured the interest of the general public.

Indeed, in some cases the arms control issue has actually subsumed foreign policy. Today progress in arms control has come to be seen as synonymous with success in Soviet-American relations. SALT I signaled the beginning of détente; the partial failure to negotiate SALT II is usually taken as marking the breakdown of détente; and superpower relations are currently being judged by the progress of START.

Yet, despite all this attention, the most important questions concerning arms control have usually been overlooked. Most discussions about arms control seem simply either to favor it or to oppose it.

Those that favor arms control usually begin by describing how terrible weapons and war are, and how the major powers have been building up their arsenals. Often these discourses refer to force levels (e.g., to the capability of the U.S. nuclear arsenal to kill every Soviet citizen ten or twelve times over), claim that the United States is about to deploy a new weapon that will escalate the arms race (in 1970 this weapon was the ABM; in 1978, the MX missile; today, "Star Wars" technology), and argue that it must be stopped.

11

Those that oppose arms control tend to argue that the Soviets are untrustworthy ogres and cite all of the aggressive acts they have committed since 1917 (e.g., the invasions of Hungary, Czechoslovakia, and Afghanistan, the squelching of the dissident movement in the 1970s, the support of Marxist dictatorships in the Third World). These discourses often go on to argue that the United States is dangerously inferior to the Soviet Union in military strength and must therefore build, build, build. Often they claim that a critical new weapon is being developed, but is threatened by misguided arms control efforts.

These debates, pro and con, are not ill-informed. In fact, few subjects of public policy are discussed with as much technical expertise as is arms control. What is missing is a basic understanding of how arms control works and what it is supposed to do. Flora Lewis, foreign policy columnist for *The New York Times*, recently observed that discussions of arms control usually concentrate too much on the minutiae of one agreement or another—whether, for instance, it matters that SALT II permitted the Soviets 308 heavy missiles while permitting the United States none, or whether the SALT I agreements really permitted the Soviets to deploy medium-sized ballistic missiles such as the SS-19. These questions are not trivial, of course, but they do tend to draw our attention away from the key questions about arms control and how it fits into American foreign policy as a whole. This book is intended to investigate precisely these questions.

Arms control must be judged by its results. Supporters of arms control claim that it saves money, reduces the likelihood of war, and limits the destruction if war does break out. Opponents of arms control claim that it does none of these things, and serves mainly to leave the United States vulnerable to Soviet aggression. These claims can be tested—in some cases by comparing them with the record of past arms control agreements, in other cases through simple logic—yet they rarely are. This book will consider the actual record of arms control.

One of the most depressing aspects of the arms control debate is its predictability. Almost before a well-known writer or official utters a word, one knows his or her opinion. The public figures who opposed the development of the hydrogen bomb in 1950 almost invariably opposed the ABM in 1970 and automatically oppose Star Wars today. The people who argued for more bombs in 1950 also argued for more missiles in 1970 and for more advanced-technology weapons today.

The consistency of these advocates is remarkable; it seems for them arms control treaties are either always desirable or always dangerous. In truth, arms control can produce a variety of results. Some treaties, such as the Incidents at Sea Agreement, have accomplished precisely what they were intended to do. Others, such as the London Naval Treaties, were utter shams from the time they were signed, and only accelerated the onset of war. Therefore, a second purpose of this book is to describe what kinds of arms control agreements are most promising, and what is necessary to obtain them.

Another problem with the current debate is its abstractness. Arms control has become a symbol. Support for arms control is a political shorthand today for favoring friendly relations with the Soviet Union and compromise with a misunderstood, slightly psychotic country. Opposition to arms control is a metaphor for getting tough with the Soviets, to check their aggressive tendencies.

Yet thinking about arms control is just an intellectual exercise unless it is in the context of the broader goals of the United States. Arms control *is* important. It shapes the tenor of superpower relations. It affects the spending of tens of billions of dollars each year. It also probably has some effect on the likelihood of war, nuclear or otherwise.

Two themes run throughout this book. The first is the politics of arms control: how to negotiate an arms control treaty, how countries usually respond to arms control agreements, and how arms control is shaped by domestic factors.

Following the signing of the SALT I agreement, many political columnists wrote that, since the first barrier to improved Soviet-American relations had been broken, we could expect the arms competition to abate, allowing the two countries to settle disagreements on such other matters as human rights, Third World affairs, and the nonnuclear military balance. As we now know, these predictions were, to say the least, optimistic. Why was

SALT I so disappointing in these respects? Why was SALT II so much more difficult to negotiate than SALT I? Should we have expected Soviet-American relations to become more difficult after the first breakthrough, or could we have done something to keep détente on course?

Following the SALT I agreements, many figures criticized Henry Kissinger for his close-to-the-vest negotiating style, which cut out many players in the American foreign policy community. Since then, the arms control process has been opened up, so no one has exercised as much control as Kissinger did. Is this change partly to blame for the current lack of progress in arms control? If so, should we go back to the earlier practice? This book will attempt to answer all these questions.

The second theme of this book is technology, the problems it has presented to arms control in the past, and the problems it will pose in the future. Controlling arms is, in large part, a problem of controlling technology. After signing the SALT I agreement, which limited strategic weapon launchers, the United States and the Soviet Union both deployed multiwarhead weapons that increased the capability of each launcher. The two countries also began to develop weapons not covered by SALT I, which complicated later arms control negotiations. The new weapons also made verification of Soviet compliance difficult. Could this technology have been anticipated and, if so, averted? If not, what problems will new technology present in future negotiations?

This book attempts to answer such questions. But before considering where arms control should go from here, it helps first to understand a little about the history of arms control.

Where We Are and How We Arrived

During the past century, countries have often tried to negotiate arms control agreements. Sometimes they have succeeded, in the sense of reaching an agreement that seemed to limit the deployment of weapons. Sometimes they have failed to reach an agreement or have not lived up to one. In any case, we have had enough experience to make some firm statements about what arms control can and cannot do.

The easiest way to understand the record of arms control is to divide the history into three parts: the international conferences on the conduct of war in the years preceding World War I; the conferences on armaments (mainly naval) in the interwar years; and the negotiations since World War II (mainly between the United States and the Soviet Union) concerning nuclear weapons.

The first modern attempt to limit weaponry seems to have been the International Peace Conference held at The Hague in 1899. One reason for this conference was the collision between the Victorian ideals of chivalry and civility and the weapons of destruction made possible by the industrial revolution. But a more important reason was simply the cost of modern weapons. When Germany and Austria bought new artillery in the mid-1890s, the Russian Ministry of War proposed to Nicholas II that Russia update its own artillery. Like leaders today, the czar was a little reluctant to add to the national budget. He was given an escape when his finance and foreign ministers suggested that Russia call an international conference to limit weapons. The Russians then invited the major governments of the world to a meeting.[1]

But the invitation fell flat. Almost every country found some excuse why it should not have to reduce or limit its armaments. Great Britain needed its all-powerful Navy to protect its trade routes, the United States was still technically at war with Spain, the French feared Germany, the Germans feared the French, and so on. The Russian foreign minister, Count Michael Muraviev, reworked the letter, deemphasizing arms limitation and stressing the need for countries to talk about the rules of war and arbitration. This letter received a much more favorable reception, and the conference was convened at The Hague, chosen because the Dutch were a relatively insignificant military power. The first session was held May 18, 1899, Nicholas's birthday.[2]

The Hague Conference did not control armaments, but it did allow the major powers to ban the use of certain weapons, such as expanding bullets and poison gas. The conference also produced the Permanent Court of Arbitration, the predecessor of today's International Court of Justice. Nations had been settling some of their disputes through peaceful arbitration for centuries, and the court was to provide them a regular venue. The rules of arbitration were still the same, though; if a country did not want a dispute settled by the court, it was not obliged to do so.

The idea of international conferences and arbitration gained currency in the first years of the twentieth century. Theodore Roosevelt, whose military credentials needed no authentication, tried to burnish his image as a peacemaker by acting as an arbitrator in the Russo-Japanese War in 1905. Andrew Carnegie, taken by the idea of a world court, donated a million and a half dollars to build a palace for the Permanent Court of Arbitration at The Hague. International arbitration began to have the same cachet as the United Nations had in the early 1950s—a civilized way for nations to do business, a better alternative than war, and possibly even a step to world government.

The Second Hague Conference was convened in 1907 at the initiative of Theodore Roosevelt and his secretary of state, John Hay. Like the first, it made little progress toward reducing armaments, but it did ban particular types of weapons (e.g., naval mines) and established standards for the conduct of war. At the time, conferences on the conduct of war were more fashionable than treaties to limit weapons; indeed, most of the leaders responsible for organizing the conferences seem to have doubted that arms limitation was feasible or, even if it were, that it would reduce the likelihood of war.

Arms control was put back on the shelf so that World War I could be fought (one casualty of the war seems to have been a third Hague conference), but afterward, both the public and political leaders were willing to give it another try. The war itself was one of the best promotions any peace movement could have. Also, some political leaders feared that the victors would start their own arms race. And munitions manufacturers—Krupp, Vickers, et al.—had received much of the blame for causing the war, so cutting their business was fair game in the politics of most countries.

Indeed, the Treaty of Versailles itself was, in part, an arms control treaty. It required Germany to remove all of its armed forces from the industrial Ruhr; prohibited Germany from having an air force; prevented the German Navy from deploying any ship displacing more than 10,000 tons; limited the German Army to a size appropriate to an internal police force; and so on. The terms of the treaty were draconian and exhaustive. They went so far as to establish a minimum term of service for members of the police force in order to prevent Germany from training a pool of military reservists.*

This disarmament plan imposed on Germany in 1919 did not work, as became painfully evident in the next two decades. The Germans evaded the restrictions through a number of schemes, and eventually the restrictions themselves became moot. They depended on the Allies' willingness to enforce them, and by the 1930s none of the Allies were willing.

Ironically, the controls may even have backfired on the Allies by aiding the development of the Soviet Army. The Germans got around the restriction against building most weapons by cooperating with the Soviet Union, the other pariah state that emerged from the war. The Soviets needed military know-how and technology; the Germans needed a place to train their own officer corps and develop their own military technology. The two countries struck a deal, and as a result, many German officers spent the 1920s in the Soviet Union, helping to organize the Red Army into a modern fighting force; to this day, the Soviet armed forces resemble the German model.†

---

* In conscript armies, such as those deployed by most European countries in the first part of this century, the standing army is a skeleton force composed mainly of draftees. All (or almost all) able-bodied men are required to serve on active duty for two years, during which time they are trained in military skills. After their term is over, they are placed in the reserves and are subject to recall. When the army mobilizes for war, it calls up the last two or three cohorts to fill out its ranks.

The Versailles treaty, by requiring German soldiers to serve for a minimum of twenty years, sought to prevent Germany from building up the necessary pool of trained reservists. Germany was able to get around this restriction by training "youth groups" that performed civic work on roads, parks, and the like, and by organizing aircraft "sporting clubs." (It was remarkable how many sportsmen wanted to learn how to fly stunts such as Immelmann loops and strafing runs.) After Hitler consolidated power, Germany abandoned such ruses and simply trained its fighting men overtly.

† The Allies were not the only ones to pay a price for pushing Germany into cooperating with the Soviet Union. Most of the Soviet officers who worked with the Germans in the 1920s and achieved higher rank in the 1930s were

The Allies negotiated a less one-sided arms control agreement among themselves a few years later, during the Washington Conference of 1921–1922. Although open to consider restrictions on all arms, the conference quickly focused on warships in general and battleships in particular. Politicians in both Great Britain and the United States feared a naval arms race with each other. They also worried about Japan, which was feeling its oats after the war. The Washington agreements limited both the number and size of battleships, but were easily circumvented. When the nations taking part in the agreement tried to patch these defects, the treaty broke down completely.

Arms control was picked up again after World War II, partly in connection with the founding of the United Nations, and partly because the United States was trying to decide what to do with the atomic bomb after having invented it. It was natural that nuclear weapons took center stage. Hiroshima and Nagasaki were proof of what even a first-generation nuclear weapon could do, and American leaders feared what would happen if other countries acquired such weapons. So, not surprisingly, the first American proposal to ban the bomb, the Baruch Plan (named after Bernard Baruch, whom Harry Truman appointed to promote the plan in the United Nations), would have simply prohibited any other country from building one by putting all nuclear technology under control of the UN.

As one would expect, the Soviet Union rejected the proposal. On the surface, the issue was one of timing; the United States proposed to disarm itself after the UN took control of nuclear technology, while Soviet leaders refused to forgo their own chances to have nuclear weapons until the United States had disarmed itself. In truth, it is unlikely that the Soviets would have forfeited the bomb until they were sure that they could build one, too. The Baruch Plan quickly disappeared.

Since then, nuclear arms control has revolved around three kinds of negotiations: controls on testing and development of nuclear weapons, such as the Partial Test Ban Treaty; controls on the spread of nuclear weapons to countries that currently do

---

shot during the Great Purge on the grounds that they had cooperated with Nazis in the past—which, of course, they had.

not have them, such as the Nonproliferation Treaty; and ceilings on the numbers of weapons that the two superpowers deploy, such as SALT I, SALT II, and the current START negotiations.

There are also regional treaties prohibiting the deployment of nuclear weapons in areas that most nations would not consider seriously anyway (e.g., the Antarctic, the seabed). In addition, there are several other treaties in force and negotiations under way dealing with conventional munitions and forces and with chemical, biological and other exotic weapons.

The record of these agreements is mixed. But the point should be clear: When we talk about arms control, we are not talking about a fantasy or an abstraction. We have had nearly a century of experience in negotiating and practicing arms control, and rather than complain that arms control is bad and misguided or good and underused, we should talk about how it works, when it works, and how it fits into American foreign policy.

So let us begin with a simple question: Does arms control control arms?

CHAPTER **TWO**

Does Arms Control Control Arms?

MOST people who support arms control today believe, at least in principle, that it limits the number of weapons that countries deploy, the development of more exotic and more expensive weapons, and hence the cost of defense. If arms control usually accomplished these goals, then no one would argue that it is not desirable. Yet just how successful has it been? And if it has not been successful, has it been improperly implemented, or is there something wrong with arms control itself?

The Recent Record

Measuring most arms races is difficult because it is hard to find an index of military capabilities that everyone accepts. However, we can reasonably estimate the pace of the current nuclear arms race by comparing the number of warheads the two superpowers have deployed; military planners think in terms of assigning warheads to targets, and in any case, it is the warhead that destroys property and kills people, rather than the missile or aircraft carrying it.

By this measure, arms control has had little effect on the deployment of arms. As Figure 2.1 shows, the United States and the Soviet Union have enlarged their arsenals of nuclear warheads at virtually a constant rate for the past twenty-five years—

Figure 2.1

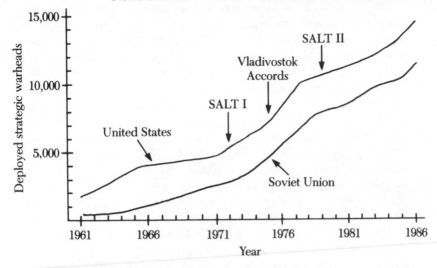

U.S. AND SOVIET STRATEGIC WARHEAD DEPLOYMENTS, 1961-1986

despite SALT I, the Vladivostok Accords, SALT II, and several lesser strategic arms control agreements in this period.*

The strategic arms control agreements of the 1970s limited only strategic weapons launchers—missile silos, missile-launching submarines, and bombers. Since both countries needed more warheads for their planned operations, during the 1960s and 1970s the United States and the Soviet Union developed various ways to deploy several warheads on each individual missile or bomber (in defense parlance, this process is called "fractionation"). They installed multiple independently targeted reentry

---

* Defense analysts often distinguish between "strategic" weapons and "tactical" nuclear weapons. Strategic weapons are those that the Soviet Union and the United States would use directly against each other; tactical weapons are the ones that each country would use on the battlefield in support of troops.

In many respects, this distinction is artificial, and probably is a result of the way in which the United States incorporated nuclear weapons into its forces as much as anything else. Though until recently they have never been the focus of arms control, tactical deployments have followed the same course as strategic weapons—steadily upward.

vehicles (MIRVs) on their ballistic missiles, and several short-range missiles on each of their bombers. Hence, the number of nuclear warheads continued to increase.

Yet, as should be apparent, it was not just the number of weapons but also the technology that grew. Arms control, it seems, encouraged the development of MIRVs and also cruise missiles. Of course, arms control was not the only incentive, but it does seem to lead countries to substitute investment in new uncontrolled weapons or technologies for investment in weapons that are controlled. The best recent example of this phenomenon seems to be the cruise missile, a pilotless drone aircraft that can be mounted on aircraft, trucks, ships, or almost any other kind of vehicle (the German V-1 "buzz bomb" was a primitive cruise missile). Cruise missiles were hardly discussed in the SALT I negotiations, and thus escaped controls.

This was understandable. No one thought much about cruise missiles in the late 1960s and early 1970s. Though the United States and the Soviet Union both deployed them during the early days of the Cold War, once each country had developed reliable ballistic missiles, cruise missiles (or at least strategic cruise missiles) were neglected. Ballistic missiles are faster and, because they fly in high trajectories outside the earth's atmosphere, they are more difficult to intercept.

Developments in technology changed all of this by the mid-1970s. Miniaturized jet engines and nuclear warheads made smaller cruise missiles possible, so several cruise missiles could be mounted on a single aircraft or ship. At about the same time, miniaturized computers made possible the development of extremely accurate, lightweight guidance systems, which reduced the advantage in accuracy ballistic missiles systems enjoyed. Moreover, these new guidance systems enabled cruise missiles to fly very close to the ground, evading enemy radar, thus diminishing the advantage ballistic missiles had in being able to penetrate enemy defenses. Since SALT I capped deployments of bombers and ballistic missiles, cruise missiles were a logical alternative. So, throughout the 1970s, engineers in both the United States and the Soviet Union rushed to develop the new technology, and by the early 1980s both countries were deploying new strategic cruise missiles.

If arms control has not limited either the number of weapons or the growth of technology, does it at least save money? Before answering this question, it is important to keep a few facts in mind. When we talk about arms control today, we are usually talking about nuclear weapons, and they are cheap—about as cheap as a well-appointed house in an upper-middle-income neighborhood. A 10-kiloton nuclear artillery shell can be bought for approximately $200,000.

Furthermore, nuclear weapons account for a rather small part of the overall defense budget. The vast majority of the defense budget goes for conventional or "general-purpose" forces, most of which are intended for the defense of western Europe, some of which are intended for use in the Third World. These forces are what economists call "labor intensive," requiring lots of personnel (18,000 soldiers in the typical armored division, or 5,000 men on the typical aircraft carrier, for example). It costs a large amount of money to pay these soldiers; about half of all outlays goes to personnel expenses.

By contrast, during the past two decades, spending on strategic nuclear programs has consumed only about 10–15 percent of the total defense budget. Strategic weapons are "capital intensive"; they depend heavily on advanced technology and require relatively few operating personnel. So one should not expect strategic arms control to save much money. Even if it did limit deployments or technology—which it does not seem to—there simply is not much money for arms control to save.

Figure 2.2 shows changes in U.S. annual expenditures on strategic forces between 1960 and 1985 in inflation-adjusted dollars. In 1962, the Kennedy Administration began what was to be a series of cuts in spending for strategic forces. These cuts reflected in part a greater U.S. reliance on conventional forces. They also reflected the pressure of the Vietnam War. But, most especially, these cuts reflected the beliefs of Robert McNamara and other defense officials who thought a limited number of nuclear weapons was sufficient to maintain deterrence.

As a result of this policy, the Defense Department imposed a freeze on the construction of new missile silos, strategic bombers, and missile-launching submarines. (Incidentally, this freeze, a sort of unilateral arms control measure, also served as the ini-

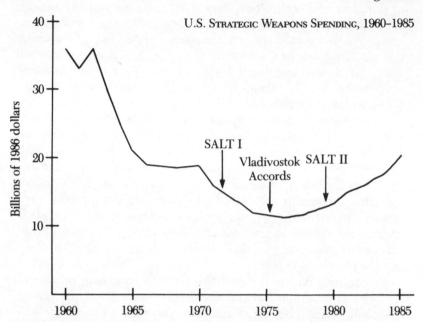

Figure 2.2

U.S. STRATEGIC WEAPONS SPENDING, 1960–1985

tial incentive for the development of MIRVs.)[1] Annual spending
on strategic programs fell by nearly two-thirds between 1962
and 1975.

Yet what was the effect of arms control on this trend? Despite
three major treaties that the United States negotiated with the
Soviet Union between 1971 and 1979, outlays for strategic weapons remained relatively unaffected, ranging between $12 billion
and $17 billion per year. Indeed, after SALT II, U.S. spending
on strategic programs actually began to *rise* slightly. Arms control seems to have had little effect on the overall pattern of U.S.
spending for strategic forces.*

In short, the record of arms control during the past two de-

* SALT II counts as a successful arms control treaty even though it was
never ratified by the U.S. Senate. The Carter and the Reagan Administra-
tions both announced that they would adhere to the SALT II guidelines so
long as the Soviet Union did likewise, and the treaty operated as though it
had been fully approved.

cades is not very encouraging. Arms control generally has not limited arms, has not limited the development of military technology, and has not reduced defense spending. It would probably be an overstatement to say that arms control in the twentieth century has been a complete failure, but it has at least been sorely disappointing by most objective measures.

A Lesson from Economics

Why has the record of arms control been so disappointing? Supporters of arms control usually say that we have never really tried it. Past agreements, they say, have left loopholes big enough to drive a mobile missile launcher through. Better controls would yield better results.

Yet what if the problem has not been the motives of the participants nor the manner in which arms control has been implemented, but rather something in the nature of arms control itself? It may be that arms control, despite the best intentions, is not the best way to limit arms.

An analogy might make this clear.

Price controls are a good example of how trying to "manage" a problem can leave us worse off than if we had simply done nothing. Most experts today would agree that, generally speaking, price controls are counterproductive. Yet this was not always the common wisdom. As recently as the Nixon Administration, mainstream economists considered price controls one of the many bona fide instruments the federal government could use to keep the economy from swinging from extremes of inflation to extremes of recession. (Price controls were sometimes called "incomes policies," because whereas controls are restrictive, policies are prudent.) It took an especially bad experience with price controls during the 1970s to shake economists of this belief.

When Richard Nixon took office in 1969, the annual rate of inflation was approximately 5 percent. It did not stay there for long. Federal spending had been steadily rising at the rate of about 6 percent per year, partly as a result of the war in Vietnam, partly as a result of the Great Society programs for food, housing, education, and so forth. Since the government did not raise taxes to pay for this spending, the costs were covered by printing money. The result was inflation; the value of each dollar was diluted as more dollars entered circulation.

The Nixon Administration's response, after studying the problem for two years, was price controls.* This was ironic, since the economic officials in the administration were almost all conservatives who had opposed such controls for most of their professional careers.

Richard Nixon announced the imposition of controls during a televised speech on the evening of August 15, 1971. At first these controls seemed to work. Inflation soon fell to the neighborhood of a 4 percent annual rate, unemployment began to decline, and the economy grew at a healthy rate.

Then things went awry. Price controls could not insulate the United States from the world economy or other events that raised the market price of goods. When an unusually bad harvest forced the Soviet Union into the world grain market, the demand for grain rose, which in turn increased the price. A few months later, petroleum prices on the world market began to rise, slowly at first, but more sharply after the Yom Kippur War in October 1973. U.S. farmers, faced with frozen retail prices but higher costs for feed and fuel, began to slaughter their stock rather than

---

* Price controls were also supposed to alleviate other causes of inflation. One was the negative balance of payments between the United States and foreign countries. The United States had been spending large amounts of money abroad, in part for Volkswagens and Nikon cameras, but also for 240,000 U.S. troops in Europe, 28,000 in South Korea, 2,500 in Japan, etc.

As a result, foreign banks were accumulating dollars. As part of the agreements made in the aftermath of World War II, the United States was committed to buying these dollars with gold at the price of $35 an ounce, but it did not have nearly enough gold to back up this commitment. Other governments knew this and restrained themselves so as to avoid precipitating a run on the dollar. But the common knowledge was that the dollar was shaky, and so foreigners were less enthusiastic about holding them.

So the market value of American money was falling, since the price of money varies with supply and demand, like other goods. Officials in the Nixon Administration knew that they should correct the difference between the market value and the official value of the dollar. Otherwise, there would be more economic problems down the road. The problem lay in how to do so without causing a major economic jolt; price controls were supposed to soften the transition.

keep it for market. The result was shortages in American super-markets.

Price controls finally ended when the law authorizing them expired at the end of April 1974. But the damage they caused was not yet over. Businesses tried to recover the losses they had suf-fered during the period when they could not raise their prices to cover their costs. Like a sealed kettle that had been kept over a roaring fire, inflation erupted to double-digit rates a few months after controls were removed.

Four years later, Americans discovered the final legacy of the experiment in price controls. The government had kept controls on domestic petroleum because some political leaders argued that fuel was too important and too basic to the economy to be uncontrolled. So oil became less profitable, and domestic oil pro-ducers cut back exploration for new reserves. When the Iranian Revolution disrupted the flow of oil from the Persian Gulf in 1979, alternative sources of petroleum were not ready to enter the market. The result was an oil shortage and a return once again to double-digit inflation.[2]

This experience should have been expected. Artificial controls rarely solve the problems presented by inflation. Instead, price controls usually just create shortages and even greater inflation in the future.

Even when price and wage controls have limited inflation, they have usually led to other distortions in the economy, such as per-verse investments, bizarre production decisions, and black mar-kets. If controls reduce the profitability of one kind of business, investors will find a new, uncontrolled business offering them an uncontrolled profit, even if the new investments are not neces-sarily in the best interests of the country as a whole. Price con-trols on oil, for example, might lead would-be oil investors to speculate instead in, say, nineteenth-century French impression-ist watercolors—a tasteful investment which might yield a profit for the investors, but no fuel for U.S. industries.

Moreover, price controls tend to become increasingly compli-cated and cumbersome over time. Governments respond to the efforts of citizens to evade price guidelines, usually by adding another set of regulations on top of the original guidelines. After a while, the official regulations become quite complex and the manuals containing these guidelines become very thick. Also, complicated rules usually require exemptions, which are rarely issued fairly.

Not surprisingly, most people seem to oppose price controls today. When the Carter Administration toyed with price controls in 1979, business and organized labor both opposed the proposal. When the administration then tried to control prices by controlling interest rates, Congress responded with a ban prohibiting it from doing so.

Most economists today do not believe price controls really solve the problem of rising prices, but for some reason most political analysts seem to believe that arms control can solve the problem of growing numbers and sophistication of arms. They are wrong. So long as the "demand" for weapons remains, arms control will not control arms, but will simply alter the pattern in which nations acquire them. A country does not have to be especially aggressive or militaristic in order to have a "demand" for arms. Some arms, of course, will always be needed simply for defense. Weapons are also political pork; elected representatives will always have an incentive to bring home military contracts to their constituents. The armed services will fight for the particular weapons that justify their existence; the Air Force will always lobby for bombers, the Army for tanks. If countries continue to have this demand for weapons, arms control will most likely cause them to find some other kind of weapon on which they can spend their money.

Usually the result is worse than what would have existed without arms control. One reason for this perverse result is that arms control upsets complacent bureaucrats. Ordinarily, bureaucracies behave "incrementally." From time to time they may adopt an innovative policy, but usually they only modify existing policies, and then only as much as is absolutely necessary. Bureaucracies exist precisely because large organizations have difficulty totally reevaluating their policies every time a decision is required.

Like other bureaucracies, armies and navies usually avoid drastic innovations. When they develop a new weapon, they usually start with an existing design, adding the new technology that seems to be profitable at the time. This bureaucratic conservatism has its pluses and minuses. On the positive side (at least from the viewpoint of opposing arms races), the armed forces ordinarily do not look for new "breakthrough" weapons; they predictably build improved versions of weapons they currently deploy. On the negative side, bureaucratic inertia makes the military less effective than it could be (as critics of the U.S. defense establishment, such as the "military reform" lobby, have pointed out).

Arms control, however, provides an artificial incentive for a conservative military bureaucracy to become innovative, shaking it out from its normal incremental pattern. It forces the defense bureaucrats to search for new, uncontrolled technology, just as price controls often lead investors to put their money into industries that they would not ordinarily support. Because of arms control, the armed forces often take a technological innovation off the shelf and develop it for use sooner than they would ordinarily, and the resulting weapons are often more deadly and more expensive than their predecessors.

The Naval Treaties

Consider the naval treaties adopted between the two world wars. In the early 1920s, the three major naval powers were the United States, Great Britain, and Japan. The common wisdom is that the policies of the three sea powers threatened to produce an arms race and that the naval treaties averted it. But this conventional account disguises the true history, which is actually an example of how arms control can produce the kinds of counterproductive results mentioned above.

Of the big three powers, Great Britain had the largest navy afloat and had already drawn plans for a new generation of capital ships. The question was how many new ships the British would build. The British, heavily dependent on maritime trade, had traditionally maintained a navy that was at least as large as the combined fleets of the next two naval powers—before World War I, Germany and France. Since the war had eviscerated the German and French navies, the Admiralty chose the U.S. Navy as the new yardstick. This may seem strange today, but the decision was understandable at the time. There was a good amount of tension between Great Britain and the United States during the early 1920s. Part of this resulted from the British blockade of European ports during the war, which had deprived the United States of much of its trade. Part was based on trade rivalry. And part was probably rooted in ethnic politics (specifically, the Irish question).

The American navy, which exited the war as the second-most-formidable naval power, had its own plans. Since the beginning of the century, the so-called Big Navy Lobby—mainly individuals interested in international trade, together with a handful of jingoists—pushed for more American warships. World War I provided the Big Navy Lobby the opportunity to achieve its goal. The German U-boat menace and the British blockade had cost American trade dearly in the first few years of the war. As a result, the Big Navy Lobbyists were able to get congressional support for the authorization of a navy "second to none." The result was the 1916 Naval Program, which would have resulted in an American fleet equal to that projected for the British. If this program had been completed, the Navy would have added a total of ten battleships, six battle cruisers, four heavy cruisers, thirty destroyers, and twenty-seven submarines to its existing force.[3]

Thus, Great Britain and the United States, at least on paper, had policies that were fundamentally at odds with each other: the British wanted a navy that was superior to all others, and the Americans wanted a navy that was at least equal to any other. If carried out, these policies defined a recipe for an arms race.[4]

Complicating matters even further were the Japanese, who were finding it increasingly difficult to support their exploding population on limited land. The obvious solution was to find more territory, and the nearest was the Chinese mainland. Indeed, Japan had already annexed Korea earlier in the century.

By the 1920s, Japan seemed unstoppable. Some of its earlier rivals—Russia and Germany in particular—had been defeated in the war. Other European countries that had been active in the Far East, such as France and the Netherlands, had been exhausted by World War I.

This left only Great Britain and the United States standing in the way of Japanese ambitions. Both were far enough away that an enlarged Japanese Navy had a reasonable chance of dominating the Far East. So Japan began a new naval construction program. Great Britain and the United States responded with plans to fortify naval bases in the Philippines and Singapore, and by increasing the number of ships deployed in the Far East.[5]

In Washington, arms control supporters gathered around Senator William Borah of Idaho, who in December 1920 introduced a resolution calling on the President to convene an international naval limitation conference. The roots of the conference can be traced at least as far back as August 1916, when Congress passed a resolution offered by Senator Walter Hensley of Missouri, who was impressed by the antiwar movements that had prospered in the Progressive Era. The Hensley Resolution declared that the Senate was in favor of convening a conference, as soon as the war was over, with the intention of establishing an international organization responsible for mediation and supervising disarmament. A year later the country was at war and the disarmament issue was moot, but the arms control movement in Congress reemerged after the Armistice, despite the success of the Big Navy Lobby in passing the 1916 Naval Program.

The Borah Resolution is a prime example of clever political packaging. It committed the Congress to reduce naval spending if the conference could settle on a limit to naval armaments; this made it possible for senators to vote for both a big navy and arms control. In addition to his own dovish supporters, Borah was backed by a coalition of fiscal conservatives—mainly Republicans, the 1920s being the age when Republicans believed in national budgets that were small and balanced—and "Irreconcilables," senators who just a few years before had opposed the United States' entry into the League of Nations. The Irreconcilables needed to show the voters that they were not opposed to peace in principle, but rather just to the threat of a supposedly entangling alliance such as the League.

This coalition of arms controllers faced two main opponents: the still-formidable Big Navy Lobby and the newly elected President, Warren G. Harding. Three years earlier, Senator Harding had voted against U.S. membership in the League of Nations;

President Harding, understandably enough, had come to a better appreciation of the separation of powers and thought it was a bad idea for the Senate to make foreign policy.

By mid-1921 a deal was struck in which both sides came away with something. Borah and his allies agreed to an additional $100,000,000 in the Navy budget, and the Big Navy Lobby and the Harding Administration allowed the Borah Resolution to be tacked onto the naval bill as an amendment.[6] (Sixty years later a similar deal would be struck when Congress agreed to fund 100 MX missiles in exchange for the Reagan Administration's acceptance of a "build-down" arms control proposal, in which large numbers of old weapons were to be scrapped in exchange for the deployment of smaller numbers of new weapons.)

Arms control advocates often tout the Washington Naval Conference as an example of how arms control can succeed when a statesman has the courage to make the bold stroke. The hero of the conference was Secretary of State Charles Evans Hughes. He believed that the United States would come out on the short end in a naval arms race. And like most foreign policy specialists then, he believed that an arms race would inevitably increase international tension.[7]

Hughes, however, had little patience with past arms control efforts. He believed that negotiators in previous conferences had become so preoccupied with minutiae that they had lost sight of the real priority, which was simply to limit arms. He also thought that his predecessors had been too willing to allow nations to complete the programs that they already had under way. "Looking at the question from every angle," Hughes later wrote, "I found no hope for success unless the three great naval powers, United States, Britain and Japan, were willing to end their competition by a determination to *stop now*."[8]

Hughes dominated the Washington Conference through the sheer strength of his personality. (It can charitably be said that Hughes did not lack confidence in himself.) Furthermore, Warren Harding—not the strongest of men—gave Hughes virtual carte blanche over U.S. foreign policy. Thus Hughes was able to plan the American opening position with the assistance of just three other men: Admiral William Pratt, a member of the Navy's General Board; Admiral Robert Coontz, the Chief of Naval Operations; and Assistant Secretary of the Navy Theodore Roosevelt, Jr. (It is mainly through Roosevelt's diary that we know about the behind-the-scenes planning.)[9] The four men knew that other politicians before them had tried and failed at arms control. They believed that their predecessors had failed because they had tried to do too much or had become preoccupied with trying to measure military power. After consulting experts in the United States and other countries (mainly to measure attitudes rather than to acquire wisdom), they settled on a plan that seemed acceptable to each of the major powers.[10]

Hughes' first goal was to get Britain and Japan to pledge that they would participate in the conference with no preconditions. He knew that once they were on board, the other countries would follow. The tension among the three major naval powers at the time made this task difficult, but after a few weeks of quiet diplomacy, Hughes succeeded by threatening to tag the reluctant partners with the onus of the conference-wrecker; by now, arms control had at least some significant support in all three countries.

By mid-October 1921, Britain and Japan had both agreed to attend. With them on board, it was easier to bring on France, Italy, and the lesser powers that had no real navies to control but were interested in limiting armaments nevertheless.[11]

The Washington Conference was convened on November 12, 1921, in Constitution Hall, the headquarters of the Daughters of the American Revolution. (In the 1920s, Washington was still a backwater town and there were no more hotels or meeting halls than one would find in any other medium-size southern town.) President Harding greeted the delegates with a perfunctory opening address. The conference selected Hughes, as the head of the host delegation, to act as chairman. He then began what most members of the audience expected would be a formal speech full of ideals and empty of specifics.

Instead, Hughes laid down the plan that he, Coontz, Pratt, and Roosevelt had devised. Britain, Japan, and the United States would freeze construction of capital ships for ten years and would scrap their oldest ships. The result would be a "5:5:3" ratio of tonnage—Great Britain and the United States were permitted approximately 500,000 tons of capital ships each, and

Japan 300,000 tons. France and Italy were each allowed 175,000 tons; this, said Hughes, was adequate because the latter two countries were primarily land powers.

The proposed agreement also limited the size of ships built in the future, again measured in total tons displacement: 35,000 tons for battleships and battle cruisers, 27,000 tons for aircraft carriers, and 10,000 tons for cruisers. Finally, the plan banned battleships from mounting guns larger than sixteen inches in caliber (the largest then deployed), and aircraft carriers and cruisers from mounting guns larger than eight inches in caliber.

Surprisingly, this proposal, once on the table, was generally acceptable to the participants.[12] There were only a few disagreements, and the treaty needed just a few changes in the weeks that followed. The disputes were interesting, however, because though they seemed innocuous at the time, they foreshadowed the strains that would eventually cause the breakdown of the naval treaties.

The first problem was the 5:5:3 ratio. Japan, the newest and most ambitious of the three great naval powers, wanted a bigger share. Hughes held firm, and the Japanese conceded the issue; U.S. officials were certain they could take a hard line because Herbert Yardley and the American Black Chamber (the first U.S. communications intelligence operation) had intercepted and deciphered the messages Tokyo sent instructing its diplomatic representatives to give in to Hughes on the ratio.[13]

The second problem was "the *Mutsu* question." Under the Hughes proposal the Japanese were scheduled to scrap the battleship *Mutsu*, which Hughes claimed was not completed and, like all other ships then being built, had to be scrapped. Baron Kato, the Japanese delegate, objected that not only was the *Mutsu* completed, but also scrapping the ship would be a public relations disaster for the Japanese government since the ship had been built with money collected through the contributions of thousands of schoolchildren.

So the Japanese were permitted to keep the *Mutsu*. In exchange, they agreed to scrap the *Setsu*, a much older ship. This concession then had a ripple effect. To maintain the 5:5:3 ratio, the United States was permitted to complete an additional battleship it had under construction. The British were allowed to replace four of their older ships with two new battleships to be built in the future. (These two ships eventually became the *Nelson* and the *Rodney*. Keep them in mind; their importance will be apparent later.)

The third hitch in the negotiations concerned submarines. Hughes originally proposed to limit Britain and the United States to 90,000 tons of submarines each, Japan to 54,000 tons, and France and Italy to 35,000 tons each. This time the British objected. They wanted to ban submarines outright. The British had vivid memories of the German U-boat campaigns of World War I, which by 1916 had reduced Britain to just a few weeks' supply of foodstuffs.

The French, however, did not want any limits on submarines at all. They had already agreed to forgo a large fleet of capital ships, and they argued that they needed substantial numbers of submarines in exchange. The French delegates had already made noises that led the other delegations to fear a walkout. In any case, Hughes was not nearly as concerned over submarines as the British were. To keep France in the fold, the other delegates eventually conceded the issue. As a sop, Lord Balfour, the British delegate, was permitted to make a speech to the conference explaining why Britain believed submarine warfare was especially repugnant.[14]

The final question raised in the negotiations concerned cruisers and destroyers, which were called "auxiliaries" at the time. In his opening speech to the delegates, Hughes expressed hope that the numbers of these smaller craft would be reduced, but he did not say how. Once again the stumbling block was the French, who wanted to make up part of their concession on battleships with cruisers. France, being primarily a land power, needed a navy mainly for harassing British shipping, and cruisers and destroyers were well suited for this.

Oddly enough, the French had the support of the British on this issue. Once France had its way on submarines, Britain decided that it needed a larger number of cruisers and destroyers, in order to combat submarines. Eventually, the members of the conference agreed to limit tonnage and the caliber of the guns carried on auxiliaries, but did not limit the overall number of such ships each country could build. The final bargain completed, the conference was closed on February 6, 1922, just three months after it began.*

The Washington Conference is the ideal that many arms control supporters hope for today: top leaders of the major powers sit together and one official makes a bold move, proposing drastic but fair cuts in the forces of all countries. Indeed, following the conference, sixty-six ships, accounting for 1,864,000 tons, were actually towed to the breakers' yards and scrapped. So, one might think, here is at least one example of a successful arms treaty.

Arms control advocates of the time certainly thought that the Washington Conference was a good idea. President Harding said, speaking at the closing session of the conference:

> This Conference has wrought a truly great achievement. It is hazardous sometimes to speak in superlatives, and I will be restrained. But I will say, with every confidence, that the faith plighted here today, kept in national honor, will mark the beginning of a new and better epoch in human progress.[15]

Hughes, not to be outdone, said in his own closing address:

> This treaty ends, absolutely ends the race in competition of naval armament. . . . We are taking perhaps the greatest step forward in history to establish the reign of peace.[16]

---

* Along with the naval treaty, the delegates negotiated two other agreements. One of these was a treaty regarding trade with China. The other was an agreement on fortifications on Pacific islands. Although neither of these agreements really had anything to do with limiting arms, they were closely tied to the naval treaty itself.

Trade interests had caused much of the tension in the Pacific, so it was important for the governments of the major powers to clear the air (or at least try to) about where one country's trading rights and "sphere of influence" ended and another's began. Similarly, there was a trade-off between fortifications and fleets: a country could not depend on using an island port during war unless it had prepared defenses, so such fortifications defined to some extent the Pacific area of operations of the British, American, and Japanese fleets. The United States agreed not to fortify the Philippines, and the Japanese agreed not to fortify any of their islands in the mid-Pacific. The idea was that the United States would be dominant out to Hawaii, and the Japanese would have free reign in the western Pacific. This allowed the Japanese to accept their lower quota of capital ship tonnage.

Outside the conference, arms controllers were gladdened. Newspapers that had supported arms control echoed the conference attenders. Two days after the final working session, the *Washington Post* editorialized:

> The world has moved forward a distinct step, not merely in the limitation of armament, but in the knowledge that a conference of nations can be held and agreements reached by the voluntary cooperation of sovereign wills.[17]

But did the Washington agreements and the treaties that followed really avert a naval arms race and reduce naval spending? The Washington Conference was followed by two more conferences, the 1930 London Conference and the 1936 London Conference (more on these in a moment). Each of these meetings produced a formal agreement capping at least some forms of naval armaments.

What were the effects of these treaties? Judging from official statistics on naval expenditures for the United States and Great Britain (the two major sea powers that took part in all three treaties), the interwar naval agreements did not limit spending on naval armaments any more than SALT I and SALT II limited spending on strategic nuclear armaments. As Figures 2.3 and 2.4 show, British and American naval spending had been plummeting for the entire period following World War I and continued to fall until 1922—the year in which the Washington Conference concluded. After that, naval spending by the two countries leveled off for a few years, and then gradually began to creep upward with the approach of World War II.

In other words, none of the naval agreements seems to have had much effect on naval spending. A cynic might even go so far as to say that naval spending was falling *until* the Washington Treaty, at which point the decline was arrested and a floor was put under naval budgets. A more charitable interpretation would be that the naval expenditures of World War I were just a blip in a long-run trend, and that after World War I the British and American governments merely resumed the naval policies they had followed before the war—gradual but steady growth.

To understand why the naval treaties failed to curb naval

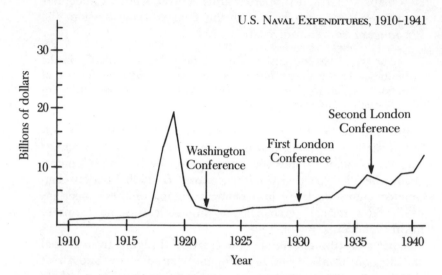

Figure 2.3

U.S. NAVAL EXPENDITURES, 1910–1941

spending, recall the lesson of price controls: as long as demand remains unchanged, a price freeze will lead producers to peddle their goods in a black market or to reinvest their capital into uncontrolled (i.e., more profitable) industries. Similarly, as long as the "demand" for arms remains unchanged, arms control only leads countries to find other kinds of arms to buy—in the case of the naval treaties, cruisers, submarines, and aircraft carriers.

After the Washington Treaty was adopted, Japan began a massive construction program of cruisers. Remember, it was France and Great Britain, not Japan, that had pressed the other delegations to leave cruisers uncontrolled, so it would be hard to argue that the Japanese negotiators were simply duplicitous at the conference. The first cruisers that Japan built were part of its already-existing naval program. The Japanese then just adjusted their plans to the new constraints; instead of building their planned number of cruisers and stopping, the Japanese kept the production lines in operation. Then the other countries followed suit.

Even more interesting is the *kind* of cruisers that they began to build. If one wants battleships, cannot have battleships, but

Figure 2.4

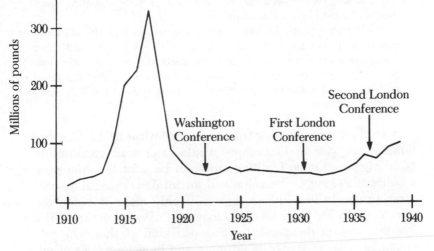

BRITISH NAVAL EXPENDITURES, 1910–1939

can build unlimited numbers of cruisers, then those cruisers will begin to resemble battleships.

After the Washington Conference, cruisers were being built largely as a substitute for battleships. The Washington Treaty limited cruisers to 10,000 tons displacement and prohibited them from mounting guns bigger than 8 inches in caliber. These limits were, in truth, quite generous; before 1922, the average American cruiser displaced only about 7,000 tons and mounted 6-inch guns. Following the conference, American cruisers averaged 9,500 tons and mounted 8-inch guns.

The same was true of British cruisers: Cruisers built for the Royal Navy between 1914 and 1918 averaged 6,900 tons displacement and almost always mounted 6-inch guns; those built between 1924 and 1934 averaged 8,400 tons and usually mounted 7.5- or 8-inch guns.[18] Arms control made cruisers bigger.

Writing in 1927, Hector Bywater, one of the leading naval experts of the time, saw the similarity between what happens under arms controls and what happens under price controls.

. . . It is somewhat ironical that a compact designed to arrest the growth of naval armament should, in practice, have stimulated the development of a vessel which has always played a prominent part in naval warfare. . . . The Conference, for reasons never explained, saw fit to establish maxima of 10,000 tons for future cruisers and 8-in for gun calibre, despite the fact that only five existing ships mounted guns heavier than 6-in.

What followed might have been foreseen. Just as the statutory maximum prices for vital commodities in Great Britain and other countries during the war period automatically became minimum prices, so have the highest Treaty limits on cruiser displacements and armament come to represent the lowest standard which naval opinion will accept.[19]

In truth, there is nothing ironic or paradoxical in the fact that limiting the size of battleships would later lead countries to build bigger cruisers. Limiting arms can be a lot like squeezing a balloon: so long as the volume of air inside remains the same, pressing the balloon in one spot will only make it bulge out elsewhere. By the same token, so long as a naval power's security interests remain the same, limiting one kind of ship will only encourage the country to build more and bigger versions of un- controlled ships. Just as the behavior of the balloon is a logical result of physics, the cruiser race produced by the Washington Treaty was a logical result of politics and economics.

There was also another place where the balloon could bulge out. Recall that the Washington agreements limited all future capital ships to 35,000 tons in displacement. But what if it is impossible to build a competitive battleship displacing less than 35,000 tons using current technology? No navy would want to waste its money on a ship that was fundamentally inferior to the ones that it would face in battle. Therefore, one would expect a navy to develop new battleship technology in order to use its allotted 35,000 tons more effectively.

This is exactly what happened. But not only was this tech- nology more efficient; it was also more expensive. The reason for this should be obvious. Suppose you are a naval architect de- signing a battleship and have to decide whether to introduce a technological innovation, such as a high-efficiency boiler, into the design of a ship. If the new technology were "cost-effective" to- day, you would use it. If you could get by more cheaply without the new technology—say, by building a bigger ship with a bigger boiler, simply substituting size for sophistication—then you might leave the new technology on the shelf. Displacement limitations, though, would create an artificial incentive to use the new technology.

Under the terms of the Washington agreement, the United States and Japan were prohibited from building any new battleships for ten years. Britain, however, was allowed to build two new capital ships in compensation for Japan's being allowed to keep the *Mutsu*. But the British were obliged to limit their two new battleships to 35,000 tons.

This was far below the size a naval architect would want. During the first quarter of the century, battleships had steadily grown. In 1900, the typical British battleship, such as those of the *Canopus* class, displaced about 13,000 tons. By 1906, the *Dreadnought*, the first modern battleship, displaced a little under 18,000 tons. Battleships built just before World War I, such as the *Iron Duke*, displaced 25,000 tons. By the end of the war, the standard size was in the neighborhood of 42,000 to 49,000 tons.

Why the growth? There were the usual political and bureaucratic reasons, of course; battleship admirals tend to want better battleships, and better battleships are often bigger battleships. However, even on technical grounds, one finds that there is a "natural" size for a battleship, and it had been growing.

Most warships are compromises among several factors: armament, speed, survivability, and endurance. The most important factor in determining the size of a battleship was usually its armament. Ship designers generally wanted to fit the biggest guns possible on their battleships in order to give them the maximum possible range; just as long-armed boxers have advantages over short-armed boxers, a battleship with a 30,000-yard range of fire has an advantage over an opposing battleship with a 20,000-yard range of fire. The ship with the longer range can shell its opponent at will, while its crew entertains itself by watching the enemy's shells fall 10,000 yards short. Bigger guns usually pack more power when they score a hit, too. The weight (and, therefore, the effectiveness) of a shell increases exponentially with the caliber of the gun. The 16-inch guns of the 1920s fired shells three times as effective as those of the 12-inch guns found on the 1906 *Dreadnought*.

The maximum size of the guns a battleship could carry was in turn limited by the technology of the day—such as metallurgy, forging, and machining. As these technologies matured, the maximum feasible size for a naval gun grew. In 1900, the maximum caliber was 12 inches. By 1920, the standard heavy gun was 15 inches, and navies were beginning to manufacture 16-inch guns.

Then there is the question of how many guns a ship would carry. There is a practical limit to the number of guns that can be put on a ship without the blast and noise of one gun disturbing the performance of a neighboring gun. In the 1920s, naval architects often debated just how many guns a battleship should carry, but most would have agreed on a number between eight and twelve.

These features determined, the rest of a ship's characteristics followed logically. One knows from the rate of fire of the guns and past experience how much ammunition a ship needs for a typical battle. One also knows how much room will be needed for the machinery of the ship and the fuel that it requires. In order to maintain formation, battleships had to keep a 20–25-knot pace, and naval architects have standardized formulas for calculating the size of the boilers and engines needed to produce the required power. The fuel requirements can also be derived from this calculation.

A naval architect did have some leeway in these calculations. For example, armor and endurance could be traded for speed; this was the difference between a battleship and a battle cruiser. But, for the most part, ships grew as navies improved their capabilities for making bigger guns.

By 1922, most naval architects believed that a battleship needed a 15- or 16-inch gun in order to be competitive. This dictated a ship of about 42,000–49,000 tons displacement. Indeed, just before the Washington Conferences the British had designed a new class of battleships, code-named the "G-3" class. As designed, these ships would have displaced 48,000 tons and would have mounted nine 16-inch guns.[20]

Unfortunately for the British, this displacement was much larger than the Washington Treaty allowed. As a result, the British had to redesign the ships in order to bring them under the 35,000-ton limit. The British did not want to compromise on the size of the ships' armament because both the United States and Japan had just built their latest battleships with 16-inch guns. Indeed, the British eventually used the guns that they had already purchased for the G-3 class in the redesigned ships.

The problem was how to squeeze a package that would normally occupy 48,000 tons into a 35,000-ton container. Sir William Berry, the Director of Naval Design, instructed the contractors who were being solicited to build the two ships to do everything possible to trim the G-3 down to size.[21] According to Royal Navy records, no other factor was as influential as the need to save weight in the design of these ships.[22]

Part of the solution was to rearrange the components of the ships. The normal British configuration for a battleship at the time was to have two turrets forward, two turrets aft, and the bridge and machinery in between; each turret housed two guns. On the new ships, the British put three guns into each turret, reduced the number of turrets from four to three, and then arranged all three turrets on the forward half of the ship. The bridge was then put behind the turrets, and the machinery behind that. This arrangement was more compact than the traditional configuration. It also allowed the designers to get by with less armor by concentrating the armor protecting the vital components of the ship into a relatively small area. This reduced the displacement of the ship further. The resulting ships, the *Nelson* and the *Rodney*, had a distinctive—and strange—silhouette. They looked chopped off, as though someone had started designing the ships at the front, proceeded backward, added an extra turret for some reason, drew in a normal bridge, and then grown tired when he arrived at the stack and simply quit. Some people compared the appearance of the ships to English bulldogs.

Even this clever arrangement was not enough, though; as designed, the ships would still have been overweight. The solution was high technology, or at least technology that was high for 1923. The most important weight-saving technology was the use of "D steel," a new alloy that was 30 percent stronger than the steel used in earlier ships. The added strength of D steel allowed the designers to cut the weight devoted to the hull structure while keeping about the same amount of protection. More weight was saved by using higher-efficiency boilers and engines. And yet more weight was saved by improving the arrangement of machinery.[23] Most of the technology had been around for some time, but it had never been worth the time or money to work it into the design of a ship until the Washington Treaty limitations increased the incentives.*

This newly applied technology, unfortunately, was expensive. Indeed, the effect of arms control on the cost and the technology of arms was profound. Plotting the costs of British capital ships from 1900 to 1945, one finds that, during the entire period, arms control was the single most important factor in raising their price.

To estimate the cost of a ship planned for construction, defense analysts usually use a statistical model based on past experience. The most important variable in these models is, interestingly, the total weight of the ship; in effect, navies buy their ships by the pound, as though they were buying hamburger. (In fact, this kind of model is used for most other weapon systems, too; today weight seems to be the best predictor of cost for everything from jet fighters to reconnaissance satellites.)

Figure 2.5 shows how the cost-per-ton of British battleships grew between 1900 and 1945. From 1900 to 1920, the unit price of battleships ranged between 70 and 140 pounds sterling per ton, with the general trend gradually upward, reflecting in part a moderate rate of inflation and in part the slow but steady incremental improvements being made in battleships. The greater the sophistication of the ship, the greater the cost per ton. (Incidentally, note that the unit cost of the *Dreadnought*, which was

---

* For example, when the battle cruisers *Renown* and *Repulse* were being built eight years earlier, the designers had considered using new lightweight machinery that took advantage of improvements in turbine design. The Admiralty rejected this proposal because of the additional time that would have been required to work out the details of the new machinery. As a result, the machinery of the two battle cruisers was an adaptation of the design used in the preceding class. The lightweight machinery would have weighed 5,100 tons; the machinery actually used weighed 6,000 tons.

Figure 2.5

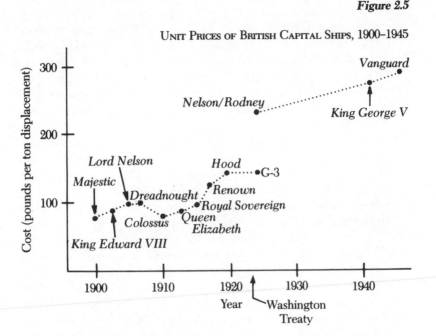

UNIT PRICES OF BRITISH CAPITAL SHIPS, 1900–1945

supposed to have represented a revolution in battleship design, was not much different from that of its immediate predecessor, the *Lord Nelson*.)[24]

Because the British government let out contracts for the G-3 battleships, we can calculate what the unit cost of a British battleship would have been in 1923 without the Washington agreements. The chart shows that a G-3 battleship would have cost about 140 pounds per ton, the same as the preceding British capital ship, the *Hood*. Yet look at the cost of the ships that were actually built, the *Nelson* and the *Rodney*—the cost per ton rose by more than a third! Because these two "treaty" battleships were based on the G-3, one can infer that most of the increase was a direct result of the technology necessary to make a 35,000-ton battleship the equivalent of a 48,000-ton battleship.

This is truly a perverse result; arms control is supposed to save money, but its main effect seems to be to make weapons more expensive. Yet the story gets worse.

Naval arms control broke down by 1937, after the Japanese withdrew from the 1922 and 1930 agreements, and Nazi Germany renounced the Versailles restrictions that limited its navy. After that time there was no arms control to distort naval planning. Yet the chart shows that, even after arms control broke down, the unit price of battleships continued to remain on the higher plateau. The *Vanguard,* constructed several years after arms control broke down, cost approximately the same per ton as the *Nelson* and the *Rodney.*

Why is this so? The answer is that, although arms control may encourage the use of new technology, the technology does not disappear just because arms control does. The new technology may cost more than the old technology, but once a country introduces the new technology, it has to assume that other countries will use it, too; once somebody shows that D steel works, you have to assume that everyone will be able to build better battleships using D steel. Even after arms control disappears, no country can risk going back to the old technology and allowing its competitors to gain an edge. Once the technology is out of the box, everyone is stuck on the new plateau—and with the higher costs the new technology brings. Thus, once arms control raises an arms race to a more expensive, more dangerous plateau, the damage probably cannot be undone.

The same ratchet effect can also be found in the strategic arms control of the past two decades. Limitations on the number of launchers encouraged the further development of MIRVs; limitations on "conventional" missile defense systems using interceptors encouraged the development of laser defense systems; limitations on ballistic missiles encouraged the development of cruise missiles; and so on.

Yet the problem is not just increased costs. After arms control encourages the development of new weapons technology, and after arms control breaks down, countries can use the new technology in uncontrolled arms. The 35,000-ton limit on battleship displacement encouraged the British to perfect new steels, machinery, and ship design. Once arms control broke down, nations were free to use this new technology in 50,000- or even 60,000-ton battleships, which were then much more effective than they

would have been if the new technology had not been available.*
And the new technology that arms control can spur on is often
more deadly or more threatening than the old technology it
replaces. The multiwarhead missiles deployed in the early 1970s
by the United States were more destructive than the single-warhead missiles they replaced, and also more "destabilizing"—more
likely to cause deterrence to fail, because concentrating a large
number of warheads on a small number of missiles reduced the
number of targets at which the Soviets have to aim. The deployment of MIRVs seemed to offer each country a good chance to
eliminate its opponent's ability to retaliate, giving both countries
an incentive to strike first.

The focus up to now has been arms control measures that are
commonly called "quantitative limits," or caps on the number or
size of weapons that a country can deploy. These measures are
probably the kind most familiar to the public; say "arms control,"
and people most likely think of turning big numbers into small
numbers. The Washington Treaty, the naval agreements that followed in the 1930s, SALT I, and SALT II were all quantitative
limits. But, as we have seen, they do not seem to work.

At least in this case, arms control supporters are wrong. Strong,
decisive leadership alone is not the solution to an arms race. Trying to control an arms race through quantitative limits is much
like trying to escape from a bog of quicksand: decisive action
just pulls one in deeper. As long as countries have an incentive
to arm, arms control merely stirs up the technological waters,
leading countries to introduce weapons before they would ordinarily do so.

If left alone, there is no guarantee that welded hulls, D steel,
MIRVs, or any other military innovations would not be intro-

---

* A similar case can be made regarding the Versailles restrictions on Germany, which encouraged German ship designers to discover some of the
most important technological innovations in military naval architecture.

For example, the Germans were restricted from building any ship having
a displacement of more than 10,000 tons. The German response was to build
high-efficiency "pocket battleships." These ships were crucial to the development of many techniques that are now commonplace in ship design, e.g.,
welding hulls together rather than riveting them, in order to save weight.

duced at some point. Yet having new weapons appear tomorrow is usually better than having them appear today.

Recently some supporters of arms control have begun to realize the problems of quantitative arms control. As a result, they have begun to suggest that we deal with the problem head-on by freezing the technology itself. Their usual recommendation is to prohibit the testing of new weapons. As we shall see, this approach has problems, too.

CHAPTER THREE

How Arms Control Defeats Itself

SOME people believe that once the ice is broken and two countries reach an initial arms control agreement, later treaties will be easier to negotiate. They are probably wrong.

This is why: By way of analogy, imagine you are a farmer. As all modern farmers know, pesticides can increase annual crop yields significantly by limiting damage caused by insects. However, if the same pesticide is used on a field for several years in a row, it will lose its effectiveness as the bugs acquire resistance.

Of course, "acquiring resistance" is shorthand; the bugs do not really become more resistant. What actually occurs is an artificial form of natural selection. In the first year the pesticide might kill, say, 90 percent of the insects. Most of the remaining 10 percent survived because their biological makeup renders them immune to the pesticide. When these insects breed, many of the offspring—a larger proportion than in the previous population of insects, say, 30 percent—will also be resistant to the pesticide because they will have inherited their parents' immunity. So, if the same pesticide is used the second year, it will not be as effective as it was the first year. The population that survives the second year will contain an even higher proportion of resistant insects, and they too will go on to breed. Each successive application of the pesticide will select out an even more resistant strain of insects, so after a few years the remaining population will be

49

composed almost entirely of resistant bugs. At that point, the pesticide will no longer be effective.

This process of natural selection works for arms control, too. When countries negotiate limits on weapons, the first round is typically triggered by a breakthrough idea that defines a "currency" or "unit of account"—a measure of the things that the treaty actually limits—which is both technically feasible to monitor and politically acceptable. In the Washington Treaty, the breakthrough was to use tonnage of capital ships as a unit of account; in the postwar strategic arms treaties, as we shall see, the unit of account was strategic weapon launchers.

Usually negotiators in the first round can cap a reasonably large number of weapons with a relatively simple agreement. Unfortunately, this cap has a perverse effect: it halts the development of the weapons that were easy to control, and frees money for use in developing other weapons that were excluded from the agreement precisely because they were difficult to control. Perhaps these weapons are difficult to locate and count, or difficult to compare with other kinds of weapons, so that a mutually acceptable balance cannot be found. Moreover, as we have already seen, arms control gives countries an incentive to develop new weapons, so in the subsequent rounds the negotiators will also have to control these new-technology weapons, many of which will be more difficult to control than the old-technology weapons. So the second round of arms control negotiations is almost always more difficult than the first. And each successive treaty will necessarily be more complex than the preceding treaty, since it will have to deal with a wider variety of increasingly sophisticated weapons. No matter how well-meaning the negotiators are, they will discover that defining a method to compare one kind of weapon with another is increasingly difficult.

Indeed, even if the negotiators are able to draft a treaty, the complexity of the new treaty will make it more difficult to enforce. Complex treaties are more likely to contain loopholes and ambiguities that make it difficult to detect cheaters or even to define what cheating is. Disputes and conflict are inevitable.

This Darwinian model suggests that most arms control agreements will follow similar paths of evolution. In the first stage, the participating countries are able to limit a large number of weapons with a relatively simple treaty. In the second stage, when the countries try to limit the weapons that escaped controls earlier, negotiations become more difficult—and more contentious. The resulting treaty, if one is reached, is usually more complicated. Finally, in the third stage, the arms control process breaks down completely when the participants find themselves mainly deploying weapons that are not easily controlled. In short, arms control, or at least the kind of quantitative ceilings that most people have come to associate with it, may be a "self-extinguishing" process.

The recent difficulties of the strategic arms negotiations illustrate this cycle. Yet stable, peaceful relations with the Soviet Union are in the American interest. So, if arms control is going to become ever more difficult, ever more controversial, and is ultimately likely to break down completely, do we want to tie Soviet-American relations to such a dubious enterprise?

SALT and START: The Self-Extinguishing Process

The movement to limit munitions came back to life almost as soon as World War II ended. In the postwar era, though, the subject of arms control was no longer battleships, but nuclear weapons. By then the United States and the Soviet Union were by far the dominant players in world politics, and both had active nuclear weapons programs; for good or bad, nuclear weapons soon became the most important measure of which country was ahead in the Cold War. Nuclear weapons also figured prominently in the war plans of both countries, so the arms control issue was regularly raised as each country developed a new generation of nuclear weapons.

The type of arms control that receives the lion's share of attention today—numerical limits on nuclear weapons—seems to have been born about twenty-five years ago. Up until then, most of the proposals for nuclear arms control were plans for strong international organizations; the Baruch Plan was an example. Such proposals may seem naive today, but world government was then a popular cause. (Even Albert Einstein and Edward Teller were able to agree on its virtues.) The United Nations was often thought to be a precursor of such a system. But even if the

United States and the Soviet Union had been able to agree on something like the Baruch Plan, it is unlikely that either would have been willing to entrust its security to an international agency it could not control.

Another problem with most of the early plans for nuclear arms control was their call for some form of comprehensive disarmament, which was patently unattainable in the real political world. The Soviet Union was especially fond of offering plans during the mid-1950s for the total abolition of nuclear weapons. Questions about how such a ban was to be implemented and verified were, according to the Soviets, "details" that could be worked out once an agreement was reached in principle. American officials, naturally, were considerably more concerned with such details. The Soviets sometimes lapse into such positions even today, as evidenced by Mikhail Gorbachev's posturing after his conversations with Ronald Reagan at Reykjavik in October 1986, and the plan he offered eight months earlier to eliminate all nuclear weapons by the year 2000.

It was difficult to argue against these proposals, as their objectives were so admirable. But timing and verification were not the only problems. The United States could not accept a ban on nuclear weapons unless something was done about the lopsided balance of conventional forces, which favored the Soviets. Soviet leaders enjoyed making their American counterparts, ostensibly in favor of arms control, squirm as they had to reject such plans.[1] But in the meantime no progress was being made in limiting the development and deployment of nuclear weapons.

Beginning in the early 1960s, some arms control supporters began to promote a different approach. Rather than trying to ban nuclear weapons completely, they said, it would be better simply to reduce the danger they posed. One way to do this was through partial agreements that reduced the total numbers of weapons and, even more important, banned weapons presenting the greatest threat of surprise attack.

It is difficult to tell who developed this idea first. Hedley Bull, a British strategic thinker, wrote about it in 1961 in his book *The Control of the Arms Race*. Another group of thinkers with the same approach, but on the other side of the Atlantic, eventually proved even more important. Not only did they develop arms control ideas; they later developed arms control policy. This group included a number of professors, defense consultants, and public officials who gathered at a series of seminars held at Harvard and the Massachusetts Institute of Technology in the summer of 1960: Thomas Schelling and Donald Brennan, academicians who studied and wrote a number of well-known pieces on arms control; Morton Halperin, at the time an academic, later a leading official in the Department of Defense and the National Security Council; John McNaughton, also later a Defense Department official; Henry Rowen, who was heavily involved in the development of U.S. nuclear war planning; and Fred Iklé, eventual Director of the Arms Control and Disarmament Agency and, at this writing, Assistant Secretary of Defense for Policy.

The themes of the group might be put as, "Best is the enemy of good enough," "What cannot be eliminated should be managed," and "Insecurity is better than no security at all." Since a final solution to the arms race seemed impossible, the Cambridge group suggested that the goal instead should be to slow the development of particular weapons that would be especially destabilizing. Assuming that neither superpower would ever really have an interest in fighting a nuclear war, such measures, it would seem, could be negotiated.

This approach was distinctive for another reason. Unlike the promoters of disarmament, who spent little or no time thinking about how their proposals could be negotiated, the supporters of the new approach spent much of their time studying the bargaining process itself. This was only natural, since the group was loaded with economists and political analysts who specialized in bargaining theory. Schelling, for example, was a political economist who came to arms control after earlier work in international economics and labor negotiations.

It is surprising how little the debate over arms control has changed from the basic issues these thinkers presented more than two decades ago. The books and articles that first promoted this new line of thinking read almost as well today as they did in 1961. For example, Brennan's *Arms Control, Disarmament, and National Security* captures most of the basic terms of the current arms control debate; it includes chapters portraying arms control as a "best available" rather than "perfect" solution, chapters on verification, on bargaining, on arms control as a means to restrain crises, and so on.

By the end of the decade, the new language of arms control became numbers and force levels, rather than abolition and supranational organizations. Instead of working toward an agreement between the Soviet Union and the United States that nuclear weapons were bad and should be banned, arms control became a process of dickering. The new goal was stability and mutual security based on some level of forces that both sides were willing to accept.[2] In effect, strategic arms control assumed the form of the naval treaties of the interwar years.

It took a number of years for the new ideas to take shape as official proposals—the Vietnam War was a major distraction—but by the mid-1960s the conditions were right for a new try at arms control. Just as the expense of weapons and seemingly insoluble defense problems drove Nicholas II to propose arms control in 1899, sixty-six years later the same two factors drove the Johnson Administration to a similar search.

Throughout the 1950s and early 1960s, the U.S. Army had been developing a defensive antiballistic missile (ABM) system. By 1965, a decision had to be made whether to deploy it. There were incentives to do so: defenses can always be sold as reasonable to protect civilians, and assuming the threat of retaliation reinforces deterrence, it is reasonable to defend offensive weapons, too. Also, the Soviets appeared to be developing an ABM of their own.

The problem was money. Secretary of Defense McNamara had already imposed a limit on the number of offensive missiles that the United States would deploy; now the money appeared ready to be diverted to defensive missiles. The potential cost of the system would run into the tens of billions of dollars—a sizable sum, then and now. The administration, already saddled with the costs of Vietnam and the Great Society, was naturally reluctant and would appreciate an alternative.[3]

For the Soviets, the time was ripe because the strategic balance had changed by the mid-1960s. When the new ideas for arms control were first floated in the early 1960s, Soviet nuclear forces were so few compared with those of the United States that the Soviet Union had neither room for concessions nor leverage with which to negotiate. This situation changed a few years later. While the United States effectively froze its deployment of new strategic weapons, the Soviets worked hard to catch up. Soon the strategic forces of the two countries were, if not perfectly equal in all respects, then at least comparable enough that the two sides could bargain.

The superpowers agreed to meet in September 1968 to begin what would become known as the SALT talks. Alas, the Soviets decided to invade Czechoslovakia in August, and American officials did not think it would be a good idea to negotiate arms reductions with the Soviet Union while its tanks were rolling down the streets of Prague. The U.S. delegation was called back just as it was about to leave Washington. The talks were picked up within a year by the Nixon Administration under the guidance of Henry Kissinger, and SALT I was signed by May 1972.

SALT I capped the number of ICBM silos, ballistic missile submarines, and intercontinental bombers the superpowers could deploy. It essentially froze strategic forces at their existing levels, though old land-based missiles could be traded for new sea-based missiles, which were considered less vulnerable and thus more stabilizing. Also, the freeze on offensive forces was linked to a freeze on ABMs; remember that this had been one of the original American objectives.

The SALT I accords, however, left open such questions as what to do about multiple-warhead missiles or missile launchers that could be reloaded. It also skimmed over such issues as how to compare missiles and bombers, or how to compare the superior size and numbers of Soviet missiles with the superior accuracy and reliability of American missiles. In addition to all of the old issues that were conveniently overlooked, SALT I also encouraged the development of new weapons, such as cruise missiles, that were to complicate arms control negotiations later.

The next strategic arms treaty, SALT II, *had* to deal with these questions—the easier ones had been settled by SALT I. One indication of just how difficult these questions proved to be was the fact that the second treaty took more than twice as long to negotiate as the first. Soviet and American negotiators began to work on SALT II just a few weeks after SALT I was signed in Moscow in May 1972, and the treaty was not completed until June 1979.*

A second indicator of the difficulty of these leftover issues was the SALT II treaty itself. By necessity, it was much more complex. In the annual summary of arms control treaties published by the U.S. Arms Control and Disarmament Agency (ACDA), the treaties, agreed understandings, and unilateral statements that compose SALT I fit into just seventeen pages. The text of SALT II, by contrast, requires thirty-three pages.[4]

The length of these treaties and the time negotiations required, of course, do not really matter. But they do reflect the "pesticide phenomenon": as arms control progresses, the remaining issues become more complicated and more controversial, not less.

One problem with SALT II was that it had to address a number of the political controversies that SALT I had created—for example, the issue of the Backfire bomber. SALT I limited the number of "heavy" bombers that each country could deploy, i.e., bombers that were assumed to be capable of carrying out intercontinental missions from the Soviet Union to the United States or vice versa. At the time SALT I was signed, these included the American B-52 and the Soviet Tu-95 "Bear" and Mya-4 "Bison." Soon after the treaty was completed, though, American intelligence analysts discovered a new bomber that the Soviets were deploying, the Tu-22M, eventually labeled by NATO as the "Backfire." From its range, it seemed that the Backfire was most likely targeted against China, western Europe, and ships off the Soviet coast. Strictly speaking, then, it was not a strategic weapon and should not have been affected by the SALT ceilings. But according to some intelligence estimates, the Backfire was just large

* Part of the delay occurred because the Carter Administration discarded the treaty outline the Ford Administration had negotiated with the Soviets. The Soviets balked at the deep reductions proposed by the new administration; by the time the talks got back on track and were completed four years later, the resulting agreement was not much different in form than the 1976 outline. Still, most of the critical issues that delayed SALT II under Carter had not been settled in 1976, so the treaty might have taken this long to complete in any case. For an account of the negotiations, see Strobe Talbot, *Endgame* (New York: Harper & Row, 1979), pp. 38–67.

enough to complete a one-way mission against the United States, taking off from an Arctic base, striking cities such as New York, Philadelphia, and Washington, and then landing in Cuba.

Naturally, the Backfire generated controversy in the United States. Many hawkish arms control analysts insisted that any SALT II treaty ought to limit the Backfire. Of course, the Soviets thought that this was unreasonable. Dovish American analysts feared that the Backfire was going to wreck any chance for SALT II. In the end, after seven years of controversy, the issue was finally settled when L. I. Brezhnev gave Secretary of State Cyrus Vance a pledge that the Soviet Union would not build more than thirty Backfires per year nor modify them so as to give them intercontinental range.

But ambiguous cases such as the Backfire were not the only problems SALT II faced. Simply agreeing what the treaty was supposed to limit had become more difficult. SALT I was relatively easy to negotiate (admittedly, it did not seem so easy at the time) largely because the two parties were able to agree on a unit of account—launchers. Although most people think that the treaty controlled arms (and, of course, they are correct in principle), the treaty did not refer to weapons as such. Rather, SALT I controlled the things that were easy to control: weapon launchers. The first section of the agreement simply says that the construction of launchers will be frozen. When SALT I was being negotiated, launchers were a reasonably accurate measure of strategic forces, just as tonnage was an accurate measure of naval power under the Washington Treaty. At the time it was not possible to launch a strategic weapon without a specially designed launcher (most missiles were too big), and it was easy to define what a launcher was, so capping launchers effectively capped weapons, too. Launchers, moreover, were easy to count.

Unfortunately, by the time SALT II was negotiated a few years later, launchers had become less important in the political debate over arms control—in part *precisely because* they were frozen. SALT I had the unintended result of providing the Soviet Union and the United States incentives to increase their nuclear capabilities while leaving the number of launchers constant. This was only natural; as we saw earlier, arms control does

not eliminate the demand for weapons. So after signing an agreement, countries naturally try to increase their military capabilities while remaining within its restrictions.

After SALT I, the Soviets and Americans stressed the deployment of multiple-warhead missiles they had been developing;
these multiplied the effectiveness of each allowable launcher. The
two nations also designed cruise missiles, which did not require
the kinds of launchers limited by SALT I. As a result, counting
strategic weapon launchers became an inaccurate guide to each
country's nuclear capabilities.

But if you cannot use launchers to define a strategic arms control treaty, what can you use? Individual missiles? If so, how can
you count individual missiles? Even ICBMs, as we shall see, can
be easily hidden these days. Do you count warheads? Warheads
are even harder to count than missiles. And once technology
creates a plethora of strategic weapons—cruise missiles, ballistic
missiles, short-range bombers, long-range bombers, etc.—how do
you compare one kind of weapon with another?

In other words, SALT II ran into the problem of defining a
currency for arms control. The old currency had to be modified,
or a new one had to be found. As with international currencies,
the "exchange rate" between, say, a cruise missile and an ICBM
is always a matter to be negotiated, and that is what the Soviet
and American representatives did—negotiate and negotiate and
negotiate.

One problem was what came to be called the "technological
asymmetries" between Soviet and American forces. Soviet ICBMs
have tended to be bigger than American ICBMs, and land-based
missiles are a larger fraction of Soviet strategic forces. Traditionally, the United States has divided its strategic nuclear forces
among a number of weapons systems—long-range bombers, land-
based missiles, sea-launched missiles, etc.—while the Soviet Union
has had a much smaller portion allotted to bombers and submarines. Each weapon system has its own peculiar strengths and
weaknesses, and this makes comparing the overall forces of the
Soviet Union and the United States difficult.

The technical asymmetry issue that plagued SALT II is a good
example of how defense decisions can have effects that lie dormant for years, only to become critical when arms control makes

them important. It is hard to say, for example, why the Soviets have traditionally built big missiles and have been so reluctant to trade them away. One reason may have been that the Soviets began to plan their first ICBMs several years before the United States did—as early as 1949, by some accounts. The first-generation hydrogen bombs were heavy, and the earliest Soviet missiles seem to have been designed with this fact in mind.

Another reason may have been that early Soviet ICBMs were not extraordinarily accurate, so their warheads—and, hence, the missile itself—had to be large, simply so they would be reasonably certain to destroy their targets. The United States was to build smaller ICBMs from the beginning because its program was begun later and could take advantage of the second-generation thermonuclear warheads—which were much, much lighter than the earlier versions—and the higher-accuracy guidance systems that were available by then. Thus, much of the difference between Soviet and American ICBMs may be happenstance and bureaucratic inertia.

Analysts also disagree about why the Soviets have traditionally preferred land-based missiles. Most defense analysts know that the Soviets developed the first ICBMs; many of them forget, however, that they also developed the first submarine-launched ballistic missiles (SLBMs). The Soviet Union converted a half-dozen of its Zulu-class submarines to carry a pair of SS-N-4 missiles in 1958, about two years before it deployed its first ICBMs and almost three years before the first Polaris submarine made a combat patrol.

The Soviets did not have a truly effective SLBM until they deployed their Yankee-class submarine (a Polaris look-alike) in 1967. They may have tapered back their SLBM program because their early sea-based missiles did not work well. They may have also appreciated the superior command and control that land-based missiles offer. Or the Soviet Strategic Rocket Forces may simply have had more clout than the Soviet Navy.

Whatever the reasons, the legacy of these early trends in strategic weapon development was felt when the SALT negotiations began (and is still being felt today). The Soviet "throw-weight advantage" caused some difficulty in SALT I, but the magnitude of the asymmetry problem did not really come to a head until the SALT II negotiations. With the development of MIRV technology—which, as we have seen, had been accelerated in part by SALT I and in part by the American decision to freeze ICBM deployments—the Soviet throw-weight advantage became important; big missiles can carry more warheads than small missiles.

The SALT II negotiators tried to go beyond simple limits on launchers and tackle the question of limiting the size and numbers of warheads, but lots of problems arose. Some American defense analysts, officials, and pundits thought it was unfair to allow the Soviet Union heavy missiles and not the United States; the Soviets, understandably, did not agree. This dissatisfaction of the American critics of SALT was illustrated most memorably by the infamous "missile board," a fixture at congressional hearings on arms control and media events during the 1970s. The missile board displayed scale models of Soviet and American ICBMs side-by-side. In their presentations, the SALT critics would first place models of the American ICBMs on the board. Then, with great drama, they would bring out models of Soviet ICBMs such as the SS-17, SS-18, and SS-19. The Soviet missiles towered over their American counterparts; the Freudian connotations can go unmentioned.*

During the SALT I hearings, Senator Henry Jackson, a leader of the Senate faction skeptical of arms control, attached an amendment to the ratification of the treaty. It stipulated that any future agreement with the Soviets (i.e., SALT II, which people were already beginning to talk about at the time) would be required to provide equal limits for both countries; if the Soviets were allowed heavy ICBMs, so would be the United States, and if U.S. heavy ICBMs were banned, so would be Soviet heavy ICBMs.[5]

---

* An article in the November 19, 1984, edition of *Izvestia* suggests Soviet defense officials have their own version of the missile board. A reporter described his visit to the headquarters of the Soviet Strategic Rocket Forces (emphasis added):

"Snow covered trees peep through the window into the office of Col. Gen. Yu. Yashin, first deputy commander in chief of the Strategic Rocket Forces. The furnishings are simple: a huge map of the world on the wall, a large globe in the corner, nothing superfluous. *The only decoration is provided by ICBM models.*"

This particular asymmetry between Soviet and American strategic forces has shaped every strategic arms control effort between the two countries to date. In the most recent START negotiations, the issue arose in the Reagan Administration's efforts to reduce or eliminate the "most dangerous, destabilizing weapons," meaning Soviet heavy ICBMs.

The technological asymmetry between big Soviet weapons and small U.S. weapons is almost always debated by asking, "Are the Soviets being reasonable?" or "Is the United States being too demanding?" Both questions miss the point. Making comparisons between dissimilar weapons is genuinely difficult—and arms control accelerates these complications. Just what *is* the correctly formulated "rate of exchange" between a relatively inaccurate, three-warhead, land-based ICBM such as an SS-11 (a light missile deployed by the Soviets in the 1960s) and a small, high-accuracy, single-warhead missile such as the proposed American Small ICBM? What *is* the comparable worth of an American cruise missile and a Soviet bomber? What *is* the "just" relationship between an American MX and a Soviet SS-18? And so on.

No perfect, objective, indisputable answer exists to the unit of account problem. But unless a way to compare such weapons that will satisfy both sides can be found, negotiating ceilings on arms will simply be impossible. Officials were willing to spill political blood over such issues in the 1970s. As strategic weapons become more diverse, the process of comparing and limiting them will become even more complicated.

Technically, SALT II was a failure; though signed by the leaders of the United States and the Soviet Union, the treaty was never ratified by the U.S. Senate and therefore never legally went into effect. Jimmy Carter withdrew the treaty from Senate consideration following the Soviet invasion of Afghanistan. To this day, there is still some question as to whether the Carter Administration could have mustered the votes necessary in the Senate. At the time the treaty was pulled, even moderates such as John Glenn had misgivings over whether Soviet compliance with the treaty could be verified. Yet any doubts that senators may have had about the ability of the United States to monitor SALT II will be minuscule in comparison with the doubts that will be raised over our ability to monitor a START agreement.

As we shall see, the weapons now left to be controlled are so small, so mobile, and so numerous that there is some question as to whether they can be counted at all with any level of confidence. Moreover, in addition to the traditional land-based missiles, sea-based missiles, and bombers, the nuclear powers are now deploying cruise missiles, highly mobile ballistic missiles, tactical weapons that are easily transformed into strategic weapons, and other systems.

The Political Consequences

No one can foretell the future, but the past does offer some hints at what we might expect if we *do* continue to link Soviet-American relations to the ability of our two countries to negotiate significant ceilings on nuclear weapons. The problems of counting, of ceilings, of finding mutually acceptable units of account, and so on are not unique to SALT and START; they are likely to occur in almost any formal arms control agreement that relies on numerical limits.

Indeed, the history of SALT I and II reflects the history of the naval treaties of the 1920s. After an initial breakthrough, the talks became increasingly more difficult, and the arms control process broke down completely when the negotiators were unable to find a mutually acceptable limit on weapon deployments.

Within a few months of the signing of the Washington Naval Treaty, the U.S. House of Representatives passed a resolution calling for new negotiations that would close what many congressmen thought were loopholes in the treaty (shades of the Jackson amendment). In particular, they wanted limits on auxiliaries, which, as we saw in the previous chapter, Japan was beginning to build at an alarming rate.[6]

Yet the second stage of naval arms control was to prove much more difficult than the first. In March 1927, Warren Harding's successor, Calvin Coolidge, invited the leading naval powers to a second naval conference in June, in Geneva, for the purpose of limiting auxiliaries.[7] France and Italy stayed home; neither would even discuss limitations on cruisers, having already given up most of their battleships. Great Britain and Japan accepted the American invitation, but the talks broke down in four months.

The problem lay in how to count cruisers. The United States needed large cruisers because small cruisers did not have enough range. The United States was late to colonial competition, and its few foreign possessions—Hawaii, the Philippines, Guam, Wake Island, etc.—were separated by wide stretches of water. So the Americans wanted to construct at least twenty-five large cruisers displacing 10,000 tons and mounting eight-inch guns, the maximum permitted under the Washington Treaty.[8]

Britain, in contrast, had accumulated many colonies around the world, so a British naval base was never very far away. But Britain also had a lot of territory to defend. The British wanted to construct a relatively large number of smaller cruisers—at least seventy ships, each displacing about 6,000–7,000 tons.[9] Yet the Royal Navy knew it could not control which British cruiser would fight which enemy cruiser. In a battle, a 10,000-ton cruiser would make short work of a 6,000-ton cruiser. So the British wanted to limit the number of 10,000-ton cruisers that the Americans could build. They also wanted to be allowed to build more cruisers than the United States in order to offset the smaller size of the average British ship. Thus the first "currency problem": how to compare a 6,000-ton cruiser and a 10,000-ton cruiser, an asymmetry like the one strategic arms negotiators face today.[10]

Finding a suitable unit of account had caused some controversy five years earlier at the Washington Conference, but the matter was still settled with relative ease. The delegates had agreed to count the tonnage of ships that each country had fully completed and in operation. Finding the exact balance in tonnage was trickier, but it was also settled fairly quickly. Yet, just as strategic launchers eventually failed as a currency for arms control, so did tonnage of ships afloat. At Geneva the British, American, and Japanese negotiators discovered that not all cruiser tons are created equal. Five 6,000-ton cruisers would probably lose a fight with three 10,000-ton cruisers. The larger cruisers would have bigger guns and greater range, would be more stable in rough weather, and would be better armored. Battleships had not been a problem, because all battleships were being designed to carry as much armament as possible, but the capabilities of a cruiser depended greatly on the specific missions for which it was built.

After the Geneva talks broke down (with much bad feeling among the participating countries), the United States and Great Britain both accelerated their cruiser programs.[11] Arms control probably would not have gone much farther were it not for the British elections of 1929. Ramsay MacDonald, the Labour Prime Minister, found that his party had lost the majority it had held in Parliament and was compelled to form a coalition government with the Liberal party. But the Liberals would not support Labour's economic program of socialism. So MacDonald turned to arms control to secure the coalition. Labour had long favored disarmament, consistent with its commitment to rolling back the British Empire. A smaller defense budget would also free money for social welfare programs. The Liberals saw arms control as being enlightened and antiwar. So under the new government the British were ready to concede to the Americans points on which they had previously been unwilling to budge. This shift coincided nicely with the election in the United States of Herbert Hoover, who, as a Quaker and a believer in international negotiation, had a personal interest in arms control.[12]

MacDonald visited Hoover in Washington in the first week of October 1929. The two leaders agreed to a proposal their aides had worked out in the preceding weeks, extending the principle of parity (the "5:5" part of the "5:5:3" ratio) to cruisers. This had in fact been the American position all along. Britain was able to back down gracefully from its earlier position when the United States agreed to a clause that allowed a country to trade its smaller cruisers for large cruisers—though in truth everyone knew that the British would not do this, and that the rate at which the ships could be traded hardly penalized heavy cruisers at all. Thus, British politics solved the "technological asymmetry" problem between the United States and Great Britain.[13]

But there were still Japan and the others to deal with. The British convened the next naval conference at London, in January 1930. Japan had been using the cruiser loophole to make up for the concessions it had made in battleship tonnage in Washington, so it naturally resisted any treaty that closed this loophole. To make matters worse, only Japan had the domestic support necessary for competing in a naval arms race.[14]

If anything, the Japanese commitment to a strong navy was

greater in 1930 than in 1927. Political luck had worked in favor of arms control in Britain; it worked against it in Japan. A downturn in the Japanese economy, the most devastating earthquake of the century, and a number of political reversals in China had all conspired to weaken the Japanese moderates. The militarists gained ground and grew even more militant.[15] Many Japanese believed their country had "lost face" by accepting a quota of naval tonnage inferior to that allowed the United States and Great Britain; they described the 5:5:3 ratio as the "Rolls-Rolls-Ford Standard." The pressure was on for the Japanese delegates to avoid making the same "error" that their predecessors had committed.

The agreement that resulted from the London Conference was not much different from the one originally drafted by the United States and Great Britain before the conference. The Japanese delegates, more dovish than their constituencies back home, gave in and agreed to extend the 5:5:3 limits to cruisers. Knowing the reception waiting for them in Japan, however, they asserted that this concession would only be a temporary measure to preserve the agreement, and that they intended to raise the issue again at the next naval conference, which was scheduled to be held in 1935.[16]

The Japanese moderates paid for their generosity. Hardly anyone today remembers the cruiser agreement reached at the 1930 London Conference. Most people, though, are familiar with the militarization that followed in Japan in the 1930s. It was partly a result of the constitutional crisis that the second naval treaty precipitated there. The Japanese Navy fought the cabinet over the treaty, and though the cabinet was able to win the short-run battle, the cost was great. Prime Minister Hamaguchi, who had represented Japan at the conference, was assassinated by a young militarist who believed that Japan had been sold out. The assassination was the prelude to the political chaos that plagued Japan through the next decade. The treaty became a bloody shirt for the militarists to wave. The Navy used opposition to the treaty as a loyalty test; officers who supported it were retired or assigned to insignificant posts. By 1935, the militarists had enough power to take control of Japanese naval policy and abrogate the 1922 agreement completely.[17]

As one would expect from the "natural selection" of issues, there seemed to be virtually no common ground on which all of the participants could agree, so the preparations for the Second London Conference took another full year, and it was delayed until 1936. The United States, Great Britain, France, and some of the British dominions were able to negotiate among themselves additional limitations on capital ships—continued restrictions on tonnage and gun caliber, for example—and hoped that Japan would go along with an agreement it had played virtually no part in drafting. Of course, the treaty was a farce. It included a clause that allowed the participants to withdraw from the treaty if another country exceeded the restrictions. Japan did, and that was the end of naval arms control. The United States and Britain were left with inadequate naval forces in the Pacific, and relations with an increasingly militant regime in Japan were strained.

The Litigious Mentality

In trying to limit the weapons that escaped control by the naval treaties, the arms control process gradually became so convoluted and controversial that it eventually collapsed under its own weight. Most people would probably agree that the current strategic arms negotiations have been in trouble, too. The Backfire controversy, the disputes over the heavy missiles, and similar episodes in SALT are well known. But the significance of such controversies is often overlooked. The complexity of arms control treaties suggests the degree to which Americans have increasingly come to think of arms control agreements as legal documents, when in many important respects they are not. Many people think that if the last agreement failed to control arms, the solution is to make a better agreement next time. But this conception of arms control attributes to it a power it simply cannot have. Domestic law can be enforced by the police and the courts. Arms control, of course, cannot.

Though arms control can allow a country to clarify its intentions and its expectations, no arms control agreement can bind a country to the rule of law. Any agreement that is reached must stand on its own, because there will be no one to enforce it if it does not. Arms control works in much the same way nuclear deterrence works; it is only the consequences that keep each country from violating the relationship. The elaborate definition of rules and obligations that become longer with each successive agreement can actually be harmful by creating the illusion that security exists where it does not. Foolproof contracts may make sense in business agreements or divorces, but they do not help much in controlling arms.

For instance, some American officials thought that freezing Soviet heavy missiles in SALT I was a significant accomplishment. The missile in question, the SS-9, carried a warhead in the 20-megaton range. According to *The Effects of Nuclear Weapons,* a handbook published by the Department of Energy, a 20-megaton warhead exploded at ground level on dry soil will excavate a crater approximately two miles across and half a mile deep. This made the SS-9, which the Soviets began to deploy in 1966, a possible threat to American Minuteman silos and command bunkers. (This was the first of the "Minuteman Vulnerability" scares.)

The American negotiators believed that, if the Soviets would limit their SS-9s, the Minutemen would be safe. By freezing SS-9s, the United States was also able to limit antiballistic missile systems, which U.S. officials had intended in part to protect the Minutemen from incoming 20-megaton warheads.

The Soviets did agree to limit heavy missiles. However, no one said anything about *heavier* missiles. While SALT I was being negotiated, the Soviets were in the process of deploying both the heavy SS-9 and another missile, the SS-11, which was about the size of the American Minuteman. The SS-11 lacked the combination of accuracy and warhead yield to threaten the Minutemen. Henry Kissinger tried in the SALT negotiations to get the Soviets to agree to a definition of "heavy" and "light" missiles, whereby any missile housed in a silo larger than the one used for an SS-11 would be considered "heavy." The Soviets refused to go along, and rather than sacrifice SALT, Kissinger yielded the point. The American side did supply its own unilateral definition of a "heavy" and a "light" missile, but this, of course, was not part of the official agreement.[18]

The reason the Soviets refused to go along became apparent a few months later when they began to test and deploy their fourth-generation ICBMs, which included two new missiles, the SS-17 and the SS-19. The Soviets designed these two missiles to fit in modified SS-11 silos. Neither was as large as the SS-9, but they were about 50 percent larger than the SS-11. In other words, not a heavy missile, just a "heavier" missile.[19]

Many Western analysts, understandably, thought that the Soviets had violated at least the spirit, if not the letter, of the agreement. (The SS-17 and SS-19 issue was a favorite topic of hawkish analysts, who alleged the Soviets had deliberately hoodwinked the American negotiators.) The Soviets, though, probably thought that the treaty implicitly allowed them to do just what they were doing. After all, Kissinger had tried to get them to agree to a definition of silo size and of limits on modification, and the Soviet negotiators had explicitly rejected it. As a result of the controversy, negotiating the next treaty became that much more difficult.

The debate was in fact over simple legalisms and the mistaken expectation that a piece of paper would force the Soviets not to do something they had clearly committed themselves to doing. If arms control is going to be considered a "legal" document, you should expect to get caught in legalisms. If you treat a complex arms control agreement like a contract, you shouldn't be surprised if the other party gets a good lawyer to find a way around it.

One of the objectives of arms control is to reduce tensions between the superpowers. Yet it seems that arms control will most likely become more, not less, contentious, and that finding a mutually satisfactory agreement will become more, not less, difficult.

If so, is it wise to make strategic arms control—or at least the traditional kinds of arms control we seem to expect from Soviet-American negotiations—the centerpiece of Soviet-American relations? It is too soon to tell whether today's strategic arms agreements will meet the same end as the naval treaties, but the prospects do not look good. If past history is a guide, it would be prudent to avoid making Soviet-American relations rest on such a slender reed.

CHAPTER FOUR

The Political Challenges of
Technical Verification

THE hopes and fears of technology meet the reality of politics in arms control and the issue of verification. At a bare minimum, any arms control treaty adopted by the United States requires the signature of the President and ratification by two-thirds of the Senate. Yet such approval is unlikely unless the President and Senate believe U.S. intelligence is able to determine whether the Soviets are keeping their end of the agreement. And in order to succeed, arms control must maintain the confidence of the American public on verification, too.

Unfortunately, the normal progress of technology, combined with the "natural selection" of past agreements, has produced a generation of strategic weapons that will confound even the most determined attempts at verification. The lightweight, mobile strategic weapons being deployed today are incredibly difficult to count; they are too small, too numerous, and too mobile. Difficulty in monitoring an agreement means difficulty in maintaining the political support arms control requires.*

* Two notes for clarification:
First, arms control experts like to distinguish between "monitoring" an arms control agreement and "verifying" an agreement. Monitoring refers to the technical process of gathering information and depends on such factors as photographic resolution, detectable communication signals, and camouflage. Verification refers to the use of this information to decide whether an arms control agreement has been violated. Verification thus involves political factors such as judgment, the willingness to risk cheating, and the willing-

Technology for Verification and Evasion

In discussing intercontinental missiles, most people probably think of the large rockets used to launch spacecraft at Cape Canaveral. Because of the technology available when they were designed, strategic weapons have traditionally been big. Even many of the strategic weapons the United States deploys today are big—as might be expected, since most were originally conceived in the 1960s or earlier.

The first ICBM that the United States deployed was the Atlas; most people will remember it as the rocket that launched John Glenn into orbit in 1962. As Table 4.1 shows, it weighed ap-

Table 4.1

SIZE AND PERFORMANCE OF AMERICAN ICBMs

	Atlas	Titan II	Minute-man II	Minute-man III	Peace-keeper/ MX	Small ICBM
Weight (tons)	130	170	35	38	80	16
Length (feet)	82.5	104	60	60	71	38
Range (miles)	5500	6300	6000	7000	8100	6000
Throw-weight (pounds)	2000	8275	1625	1975	8000	1100
Year Deployed	1959	1962	1964	1974	1986	1990

proximately 130 tons. The second American ICBM, the Titan, weighed 170 tons. Although bigger, from a technical point of

ness to suffer the political fallout of an accusation of a violation. Verification is monitoring capability multiplied by politics.

Second, some people associate high-technology weaponry with space-based defensive systems, energy beams, and antisatellite weapons. These may prove difficult to control but are, in truth, still ten to fifteen years in the future.

view it was really not much different from the Atlas; its greater size was a result of its payload, which was more than four times greater. Both the Atlas and Titan were so big that they required massive concrete-and-steel launching pads or silos, as well as elaborate ground support facilities for their difficult-to-handle liquid propellants (kerosene and liquid oxygen in the case of the Atlas; hydrazine, unsymmetrical dimethylhydrazine, and nitrogen tetroxide in the case of the Titan).

Later American ICBMs have been more efficient and, for the most part, smaller. The next-generation ICBMs, the Minuteman, for example, weighed in the neighborhood of 35–40 tons, depending on the model. And the planned "Small ICBM" (known in the press as the "Midgetman") will be able to carry out the same mission as the Minuteman, delivering a medium-sized warhead to another continent, while weighing only half as much as current single-warhead ICBMs.*

The same trend is true for cruise missiles. The United States deployed its first cruise missile, the Matador, in 1948. In many respects, it was like an unmanned version of an early jet fighter; the weapon weighed nearly seven tons. Today, a cruise missile such as the GLCM (ground-launched cruise missile) weighs less than one-fourth as much as the Matador and is much smaller. These small cruise missiles can be mounted on almost any airplane, truck, or ship.

These trends, of course, do not apply just to American weapons. The Soviet Union is developing its own versions of each of these small weapons, and even seems to be slightly ahead of the United States in some areas. In late 1985, for example, the Soviets

---

* The exception to this trend toward smaller missiles is the MX, which the United States is now deploying in old Minuteman silos. The MX, though, is big mainly because of politics, not technology. After the Soviets began to deploy the SS-17 and SS-19, American officials decided that they would beat the Soviets at their own game—if the Soviets had established that a "bigger" missile (i.e., larger than an SS-11 but smaller than an SS-18) was permissible under SALT I, then the United States could build such a missile, too. The answer was the MX, which is as big as the SS-19 but has the ten-warhead capability of the SS-18. Unfortunately, this reasoning has backfired, for the MX is so big that it cannot easily be deployed on a mobile launcher. Short of this kind of perverse political reasoning, however, there is no reason why a modern ICBM should not be small.

Table 4.2

SIZE AND PERFORMANCE OF AMERICAN CRUISE MISSILES

	Matador	GLCM
Weight (pounds)	13,800	3200
Length (feet)	39.6	20.3
Wingspan (feet)	28.7	8.2
Range (miles)	600	2000
Deployment (year)	1949	1983

deployed their SS-25, a missile that is about as mobile as the Midgetman will be. The Soviets also have a cruise missile, the SS-N-21, which is about the same size and weight as the American GLCM. It is intended for use in submarines, but like the American cruise missile, it can also be mounted on trucks, surface ships, or airplanes.[1]

These new weapons are incredibly difficult to locate and count through intelligence methods, or what Soviet-American arms control agreements obliquely label "national technical means." Monitoring an arms control agreement based on numerical ceilings is literally a matter of sitting down with photographs taken from a reconnaissance satellite and counting the number of missile silos in the Soviet Union, or the number of missile-launching submarines as they are rolled out of Soviet construction halls. Small weapons are easily hidden and are so mobile that it is difficult to keep a running count of them after they are deployed.[2]

In truth, the technological advantage between hunting and hiding weapons has swung back and forth. Reconnaissance technology, like weapon technology, has developed steadily over the years. The first airborne photographer, a French balloonist named Gaspard-Felix Tournachon, sent a camera aloft as early as 1858. Tournachon, who went by his pseudonym, Nadar, was mainly interested in surveying land without having to drag along the usual equipment. Military officials, of course, are also interested in surveying land (as well as what is crawling on top of it), so Nadar was soon approached by Napoleon III, who had a considerable interest in knowing what was on the other side of the hill. Alas, Nadar was a pacifist.[3]

Aerial reconnaissance had to await the invention of the airplane to become truly practical, but Wilbur Wright took a photographer for a ride in an airplane in 1908, just five years after he and Orville made their first flight. Italy was the first country to fly photoreconnaissance missions in wartime (against Turkey, in 1911), and most countries that had air forces conducted at least some aerial reconnaissance in World War I and World War II.

After World War II, the lack of Western intelligence on the Soviet Union was remarkable (the Russians had built entire industrial cities east of the Urals that were unknown to the West), and the United States and Great Britain turned to aerial reconnaissance to fill the gap. The British tried first, flying modified Canberra bombers from Germany to Iran in the early 1950s; these missions obtained the first photographs of the new test centers the Soviets had built at Kapustin Yar and Tyuratam. But the flights set off alarms at Soviet fighter bases all along the way, and so the British decided not to push their luck and discontinued the missions.[4]

These early attempts eventually led to the famous U-2 project, which provided the United States with photography of Soviet missile bases and other military installations during the last half of the 1950s.[5] The U-2s had operated successfully for almost four years when, in May 1960, the Soviets demonstrated by downing Francis Gary Powers near Sverdlovsk that their newly developed surface-to-air missiles could destroy even high-altitude aircraft. Again the technological advantage went to the hiders.

The technology that returned the advantage to the hunters was the orbiting satellite. The prototype of the first U.S. reconnaissance satellite, operated as the *Discoverer* program, was launched just a little more than a year after the first American satellite was orbited. By the early 1960s, the U.S. intelligence community was collecting satellite imagery on a regular basis. Today, reconnaissance satellites, both military and civilian, are commonplace.[6]

Yet, as remarkable as reconnaissance satellites are, they still have their limitations. One is their ability to locate and identify objects adequately; some objects may be too small. For example, according to one study, nuclear weapon components can be "detected" with a camera system having an eight-foot resolution; "precise identification" requires a resolution of one foot; and "technical information" requires a resolution of six inches.[7] (Nuclear warheads these days tend to be about a foot-and-a-half long and a foot in diameter.) So one can imagine the difficulty distinguishing between, say, a nuclear artillery shell and a conventional round. Moreover, even with very powerful photographic systems, an object can evade detection simply by being kept inside a building or transported in a nondescript vehicle.

Another limitation is the amount of territory a satellite can photograph on a single pass and how often it passes over a given point. Contrary to what many people think, reconnaissance satellites do not allow the United States to peer into any point of the Soviet Union at will. Unlike communications satellites, which "hover" over one spot in a geosynchronous orbit, the typical photoreconnaissance satellite "skims" over the earth in an orbit about 100 miles high and requires about ninety minutes to complete one orbit. (A geosynchronous orbit requires an altitude of about 24,000 miles, much too high for useful intelligence imagery.) Photoreconnaissance satellites are launched into "polar" (i.e., north-south) orbits, so that as they orbit and the earth rotates underneath, a satellite tracks across successive slices of the globe.[8]

The interval between the occasions at which a satellite flies over a specific target is called the satellite's "revisit time." When revisit time is compounded by interference from darkness and cloud cover, it is possible that days, weeks, or even months may pass before a reconnaissance satellite can take a second look at a given location. Since a large truck carrying a missile can travel at least thirty to forty miles per hour over a road in reasonable condition, the new small ICBMs and cruise missiles can easily beat the "information cycle" of a satellite. The problem, of course, is much worse when tracking the movements and positions of several hundred launchers.

Moreover, it is theoretically possible to fire off a modern solid-fueled ICBM without a launcher, so launchers may no longer even be a valid currency for arms control. This issue arose before, when opponents of SALT II, such as Paul Nitze, argued that the treaty was flawed because it limited only launchers, not missiles. The Soviets, these critics said, probably had saved some of the old missiles they were required to deactivate under SALT I, even though they had destroyed their silos. Despite the warning, this issue really was unimportant at the time, because it was unlikely any of these delicate, liquid-fueled missiles could be used without the launching pads or silos for which they were designed. Moreover, most of these missiles did not have a long shelf life; their fuels were highly corrosive, which would have worn out their pumps and plumbing.*

Nowadays, though, launchers are less of a constraint. Small ICBMs can be kept inside the factory until they are ready for use, or they can be hidden inside ordinary trucks. And whereas the older missiles were liquid-fueled and thus required a lot of ground support equipment, most modern missiles are solid-fueled and need few ground facilities; just prop them up and let them go. In an emergency, they can probably be used even without a specially designed launcher. (The U.S. Air Force actually did this with one of its Minuteman ICBMs in 1979.)

So counting weapons has become more difficult as they have matured. As a result, our confidence in our intelligence estimates of Soviet forces, and our ability to verify Soviet compliance with arms control, will diminish. Indeed, this has been apparent since the Soviet Union deployed its mobile, solid-fuel SS-20 intermediate-range missile in 1977. The Department of Defense officially estimated in 1986 that the Soviets had deployed 441 SS-20 launchers, with one reload for each launcher.[9] This would have yielded a total of 882 missiles that could be launched on short notice by the forces in the field. Yet the Defense Department

* The SALT II critics should have known this. Even while they were making their argument, the Air Force was having epic difficulties with its own liquid-fueled Titan II missiles, which had been deployed at about the same time as the Soviet missiles were dismantled to comply with SALT I. The Titans had been kept as bargaining chips, but deteriorated during the 1970s and were continually giving the Air Force problems. As the result of a fuel leak, one spewed noxious fumes over a wide area in Kansas. Another Titan, based near Little Rock, Arkansas, exploded in 1979 when a crewman dropped a socket wrench while working in a silo; the wrench punctured the side of the missile, the volatile fuel spilled out, and the silo and missile were history. Soon after, the Air Force decided to deactivate the Titans.

does not say how it arrived at the "one reload per launcher" figure. It might be based on estimates of possible SS-20 production. Or the estimate might be based on some other kind of reporting. Whatever the case, according to Department of Defense drawings, the garages used to house SS-20 mobile launchers are clearly big enough for several SS-20s, and it would not be difficult for the Soviets to stockpile missiles in warehouses, barns, or just in the extra space at the SS-20 factory.[10] The figures given for SS-20 deployments would therefore seem to be considerably less reliable than a count of missiles that require a fixed silo.*

Some Soviet spokesmen indicated in early 1987 that the Soviet Union would accept some form of "on-site" inspection. But how much inspection is enough? Since modern ICBMs are small enough to hide inside the factories that manufacture them, it would seem that the U.S. inspectors would have to visit the factories and count the missiles as they come off the assembly line. Which raises an interesting question: would American missile contractors allow *Soviet* inspectors inside their factories to verify an arms control agreement?

This problem is even more relevant for cruise missiles. Cruise missile launchers are small enough to be mounted on almost any vehicle. Moreover, cruise missiles are so small and light that they can be hidden almost anywhere; even the production facilities could probably be disguised. Not surprisingly, the U.S. government to date has not even attempted to provide public estimates of the Soviet cruise missile force, and neither the Soviets nor the Americans have proposed how cruise missile production could be monitored.

Yet these technical developments are only one half of the difficulty that arms control must face today. The other half of the

---

* For example, following the signing of the Vladivostok Accords, Henry Kissinger observed:

"The factor of confidence we have with respect to land-based mobiles [i.e., mobile missiles] is, of course, much less than it is with respect to land-based fixed. In land-based fixed, we have almost 100 percent confidence. In land-based mobiles, we could be off by some 25 percent."

See U.S. Department of State, Bureau of Public Affairs, "Background Briefing of Secretary of State Henry A. Kissinger, 3 December 1974," cited in Roger P. Laurie, ed., *SALT Hand Book: Key Documents and Issues, 1972–1979* (Washington, D.C.: American Enterprise Institute, 1979), p. 305.

verification equation is politics, which explains not only how the verification issue will determine the feasibility of arms control, but also why it is inevitable that the verification issue will be raised.

The Domestic Dimension

By 1980, the SALT II treaty had survived almost eight years of negotiation and had been approved by the leaders of both the United States and the Soviet Union, only to run up against a recalcitrant U.S. Senate. In the end, the one hurdle SALT II failed to clear was the American political system. The Senate did not actually reject the treaty; President Carter withdrew SALT II from consideration as a response to the Soviet invasion of Afghanistan. Still, there is some question as to whether the treaty would have received the necessary votes. Even moderates within Carter's own party had reservations concerning the ability of the United States to monitor Soviet compliance. If the Senate had approved SALT II, it probably would have added a number of qualifications and amendments that would have called the treaty's validity into question. (Some of the proposed changes were called "killer amendments," because they were specifically intended to gut the treaty or to elicit rejection by the Soviets.) The difficulties of SALT II were amply demonstrated during the 1980 presidential campaign when Ronald Reagan successfully ran on a SALT-bashing platform.

The merits of SALT II aside, can any arms control treaty survive democracy? Obviously, arms control requires a good amount of public support to succeed in a democracy, and riskier treaties satisfy smaller portions of the electorate. Yet arms control faces other problems from democratic government, too, and these are just as important as the art of negotiating with the Soviet Union or the technology of the reconnaissance systems used to monitor the agreement; unless they are solved, no arms control is possible.

One reason the United States has such difficulty in developing a consistent, reasonable arms control policy is that large, diverse democracies almost always lack a stable consensus on broad, complex issues. Obtaining agreement on just the beginning questions of arms control, such as whether it is good or bad, is difficult enough. Reaching a consensus on a specific, tangible agreement is even more daunting. As a result, the United States has great difficulty in setting out an arms control policy for itself, let alone negotiating it with another country.

The nuclear freeze movement of the early 1980s, for example, was a direct response to the complications modern mass politics poses to arms control. Supporters of arms control believed that it had become so complicated by esoterica such as throw-weight, warhead counts, and definitions of "strategic nuclear delivery vehicles" that they had lost the public's attention. So they decided to simplify the issue.

The freeze idea seems to have originated with Roger Mollander, a former adviser to Jimmy Carter. Rather than being preoccupied with the details of defining which weapons would be limited under an agreement and the levels at which they would be limited, Mollander said the United States and the Soviet Union should simply stop *all* further development and deployment of nuclear weapons.

The idea did have a certain appeal. Most of the public believed that both the Soviet Union and the United States had many more nuclear weapons than they could ever use in any war. The intricacies of targeting, which drive the "requirements" for thousands of weapons, are an insider's game that the public does not care about. (They have a point; try explaining why within a given Soviet city military planners designate a dozen individual targets, assigning each its own nuclear weapon.) After the failure to ratify SALT II—as complex and arcane an agreement as two countries have ever negotiated—the freeze seemed like a reasonable alternative.

The freeze movement was strong in 1981 and most of 1982, and probably reached its high-water mark in June 1982, when supporters staged a mass demonstration in Central Park. It was the largest such event in New York City's history; almost a million people marched to hear the predictable speakers: Barry Commoner, Ralph Nader, Jane Fonda, and so on. Yet, within six months, the freeze movement had almost vanished. Why?

One reason was that freeze proposals were popular when they

were new and ambiguous, but lost support once their details were made clear. Some of the more extreme "freezers" believed that the United States should simply stop building nuclear weapons, no matter what the Soviet Union did; this was the "unilateral freeze" version. Other advocates believed that the Soviet Union and the United States should both stop building nuclear weapons; this was the "mutual freeze" version. Still other supporters believed that the Soviets and Americans should negotiate an agreement prohibiting the deployment of new weapons, while permitting each side to verify the other's compliance; this was the "mutual and verifiable freeze" version.

Alas, not everyone in the freeze movement could live with their partners' definitions. The extreme elements thought the verification requirement was a cop-out, since almost everyone agrees verifying a total freeze of Soviet nuclear deployments is next to impossible. But freezers who were political professionals knew supporting any agreement that depended on Soviet goodwill was political suicide.

The Democratic party endorsed the freeze early in the movement, but after the problems became apparent, the party inched away from its earlier position. By the summer of 1984, when Walter Mondale, the Democratic party's presidential nominee, described what he thought a freeze would entail, it amounted to not much more than a SALT I-style limit on the deployment of missile launchers and bombers. By the November election even this tepid freeze was almost irrelevant. Yet what happened to the freeze is what happens to most arms control proposals if they are subjected to mass democratic politics. Any concrete proposal becomes a target at which opponents will inevitably shoot. If the opponents are patient, the coalition supporting the agreement will eventually begin to fray.

Many arms control supporters like to quote Dwight D. Eisenhower's observation that "people want peace so much that one of these days government had better get out of their way and let them have it." They imply that the common man favors arms control and that it is only the "elites" who are to blame for the arms race. Arms control supporters also cite evidence from public opinion polls. For example, the results of one of the most recent polls, taken by the Yankelovich organization, were published in the fall 1984 issue of *Foreign Affairs*. At first glance, the results suggest that about three-fourths of the American public favors an arms control agreement with the Soviet Union. (The exact figure depended on just how the question was phrased in the survey.)

Yet the support for arms control is not nearly as deep as one might think—or, at least, not so deep that political leaders can paper over the difficulties negotiating arms control really poses. At the height of the nuclear freeze campaign, CBS and *The New York Times* surveyed the public on arms control. Like the Yankelovich survey, they found that about three-fourths of the public (77 percent) supported a nuclear freeze. Indeed, most other polls taken during the past two decades have produced about the same result. However, when the pollsters modified the question to "Would you support a nuclear freeze if either side were able to cheat without being detected?" or "Would you favor a nuclear freeze if it failed to stop the Soviet Union from deploying additional weapons?" the results of the poll flip-flopped: about three-fourths of the sample *opposed* arms control. Interestingly, about two-thirds of the people interviewed for this poll believed that the Soviet Union would indeed cheat on an arms control agreement.[11]

These results make the collapse of the freeze movement—and other arms control movements—easier to understand. Public support for arms control is broad, but it hinges on a number of qualifications. If an arms control proposal is exposed to public scrutiny for any length of time, eventually the debate will reveal any flaws in it. These flaws drain support, so that the arms control proposal that American democracy favors today will be the one it rejects tomorrow.

The reason democratic debate will keep probing so persistently for any flaw in an arms control agreement is that political competition demands it. The key to winning in democratic contests is to split apart the opposition by framing issues so that the flaws in its policies can be seen clearly.

Politicians have little time to *change* the opinions of the public. They therefore take the public's attitudes on the issues as a "given," and search—at least intuitively—for issues that cater to their existing attitudes.* This is why the verification issue will inevitably be raised in any debate concerning arms control. Though most Americans favor arms control in principle, as we have seen, they do not favor it if the Soviets would be able to cheat. And, as we have also seen, most Americans believe that the Soviets are prone to cheating. Ergo, a politician opposed to arms control does not have to argue that a proposed treaty is bad; indeed, it would be foolish to do this, because Americans are inclined to favor arms control. Instead, he simply needs to argue that the treaty will allow the Soviets to cheat. The verification issue, if properly used, can devastate arms control, which is precisely why it will always be raised. This strategy is even more viable now that verification is in fact becoming more difficult.

Moreover, as important as arms control may be, it is still just one issue in the larger game of American politics. The number of politicians who adopt arms control (or any other specific issue) as their pet interest is always just a fraction of the total. So, to gain support, advocates and opponents of arms control must both be willing to "logroll" with their colleagues. Such dealing can suck arms control into political controversies with which it has little connection. A politician may care little about controlling nuclear weapons in comparison with, say, keeping price supports for soybeans. An opponent of arms control thus might be able to trade his vote for soybean supports in exchange for his colleague's vote against, say, a comprehensive nuclear test ban. In this way, arms control can become a casualty of a drought in the Midwest. (Indeed, the United States shifted to a more hard-line stance in the 1970s partly because arms control opponents wove the verification issue into the fabric of other conservative issues.)

Of course, not every allegation of Soviet cheating is just a cyni-

---

* Studies suggest that most people do not change their basic beliefs on basic issues of war, peace, equality, justice, etc. (There are, of course, exceptions— e.g., former weapons scientists Herbert York and Andrei Sakharov, who have become avid proponents of arms control—but they are not the norm.) This is why mass changes in public attitudes are usually more the result of demographics than of propaganda; as Voltaire said, "It requires ages to destroy a public opinion."

cal political maneuver. It is precisely because the Soviets have violated at least some arms control agreements that the verification issue is so powerful. Still, democracy and technology guarantee that the verification issue will be raised. So it is not enough to find a reasonable arms control plan and then negotiate it with the Soviets. Any American strategy for arms control must consider American politics. The freeze marchers in 1982 seem to have believed that they could convince the public that arms control was desirable and that this in itself would produce an agreement. The merits of the freeze aside, the fact remains that polemics are not enough.

Verification: The Problem of Planning

Other features of American democracy can also complicate the long-term planning necessary for verification of arms control. "Checks and balances" and "separation of power" may seem like civics-book abstractions, but, in fact, they can create major problems. For example, a reasonable approach for limiting, say, ICBMs would be first to decide which characteristics of an ICBM can be monitored, then to negotiate a treaty that limited these characteristics, and finally to deploy the intelligence systems necessary to monitor the agreement. Yet this is not how our government operates.

Within the executive branch alone, the planning of verification proposals and the intelligence systems necessary to carry them out is divided among the Department of State and the Department of Defense; the Arms Control and Disarmament Agency; the White House, with the National Security Council staff; and the intelligence community. The legislative branch also has its authority; the Senate and the House each have some say over arms control, and, within each chamber, authority is further divided among the committees responsible for the armed services, appropriations, and intelligence. And in addition to all of the governmental bodies, there are nongovernmental players: lobbies that promote and oppose arms control; corporations that have an interest in which weapons are built and which are canceled; religious groups that perceive arms control as a test of America's willingness either to reject war or to resist Communism; newspapers and television; academics; and so on. It is difficult to move such a collection of bodies in unison.

Ironically, among all of these organizations, the ones most responsible for monitoring arms control often have the least to say about it. For example, the U.S. negotiating position in the START negotiations in Geneva is formulated by the Special Arms Control Advisory Group (usually called SAC-G), a small set of high-ranking officials from the State Department, the Defense Department, and the National Security Council who meet regularly at the White House. Unfortunately, the people with the job of studying verification are about a mile to the west, at the State Department, where the Assistant Director for Verification and Intelligence works at the Arms Control and Disarmament Agency (ACDA). The physical distance is not important (it costs $2.10 by taxi); the bureaucratic distance is. The Assistant Director for Verification and Intelligence—the only official in the entire government, incidentally, with the word "verification" in his title—is separated by three layers of bureaucracy from where the policy is being developed.

As a result, SAC-G formulates the U.S. negotiating position *first,* and *then* decides how (or even whether) the resulting agreement could be verified. SAC-G includes a representative from the CIA's Arms Control Support Staff, whose job it is to give the panel an estimate of whether a proposed agreement could be verified and the degree of risk entailed, but this advice is almost entirely of a technical nature—and, in any case, verification is an after-the-fact consideration.

Even farther removed are the intelligence systems necessary for verification, which are planned by committees in the Intelligence Community Staff, the organization that acts as a secretariat for the Director of Central Intelligence. Photographic reconnaissance satellites, for example, are planned by the Committee on Imagery Exploitation, or, as it is known within the intelligence community, COMIREX.[12] The members of COMIREX are drawn mainly from the agencies that operate the satellites, along with some of the agencies that use the product. But ACDA is not a regular member of the committee, and even when it is represented at the committee's meetings, its arguments in favor of one system or another under consideration are just one voice among many.

The result is what one might expect: the needs for monitoring arms control get lost. Of course, the country can spend only so much on intelligence, and arms control, though a real concern, is not necessarily the most pressing concern. And, admittedly, the politics of arms control are at odds with the planning necessary for intelligence systems; a major intelligence system can require five years or more from inception to deployment, during which time the negotiating position of the United States could have shifted a half-dozen times. Yet the central problem remains: the connection between U.S. capabilities to monitor arms control and the formulation of U.S. arms control policy is a loose one at best.

Verification and Credibility

Another difficulty democratic politics poses is the seeming inability to act upon evidence of a violation. Twenty-five years ago, when the current arms control movement was just getting under way, Fred Iklé wrote an article pointing out that the ability to monitor an arms control agreement is irrelevant if a country is unable or unwilling to respond to a violation. He observed that if a Soviet-American arms control treaty were to work, the United States had to convince the Soviet Union that, if they violated the agreement, the United States would retaliate, most likely by rejecting arms control.[13]

The article was entitled, "After Detection, What?"; the question never has been answered well. The most obvious response would be to abrogate the agreement and build more weapons. Yet can the United States do so? Not once during the postwar period has the American public supported a sustained military buildup. Historically, any military buildup has soon acquired enough opposition to extinguish it after only five or six years.

This is clear from a quick look at U.S. military spending and public support for defense. As Figure 4.1 shows, despite the complaints of both hawks and doves, U.S. defense expenditures (adjusted for inflation) have remained more or less constant for

Figure 4.1

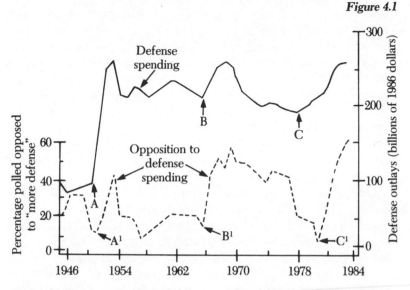

Since the Korean War, U.S. defense spending has hovered in a relatively narrow range—about $190 to $260 billion in inflation-adjusted dollars.

Each time defense spending rose, popular opposition to defense rose, too. Point A indicates when defense spending began to rise for the Korean War; Point B indicates when defense spending began to rise for the Vietnam War; and Point C marks the beginning of the defense buildup begun by Jimmy Carter and continued by Ronald Reagan.

"Opposition to defense spending" is taken from polls conducted by George Gallup; the figures for 1965–1968 are estimates based on attitudes toward U.S. support for the war in Vietnam, as Gallup's surveys focused on the war during those years.

almost four decades. With the onset of the Cold War, defense outlays rose to an average level of about $230 billion per year, and have varied not more than 10 or 12 percent from this range since. (Currently we are at the high end of the range.)

What is even more interesting, though, is the relationship of public opinion to defense spending. As the diagram shows, each time defense spending began to rise, public support for cutting defense spending also began to rise. (And, as one would expect from this pattern, now that defense outlays are at the high end of the postwar range, so is public support of defense cuts.) In other words, four decades of experience suggests that the United States simply will not support annual defense budgets much above $260 billion for any length of time—regardless of whether or not the Soviets violate an agreement.

Indeed, in almost every country with a democratically elected government, the trend is the same, and defense spending, adjusted for inflation, has remained relatively flat for the past two decades. It seems that nothing short of a major, epoch-ending event, such as World War II or the crises marking the onset of the Cold War, is able to upset these patterns. As a result, Western democracies have usually been paralyzed, unable to respond to even the most blatant arms control violations.

One of the best historical examples is the case of the Italian cruiser *Gorizia*. Throughout the 1920s and 1930s, Western naval experts suspected that Germany, Japan, and Italy were building cruisers that exceeded the 10,000-ton limit imposed by the Washington Treaty. For years, however, no one could prove this conclusively. It is difficult to calculate precisely the displacement of a ship observed from a distance, and the leaders of the democracies feared causing an international crisis.

Then, in August 1937, the *Gorizia* was heavily damaged by an internal explosion and was towed to Gibraltar, the nearest port capable of making repairs. While the ship was in dry dock, the British engineers thought they might as well inspect the cruiser to see if their suspicions were true. So they analyzed its design and even took precise measurements of the ship. As they expected, the British found that the cruiser's displacement was at least 10 percent greater than the limit set by treaty. In other words, the British had the evidence of the Italian violation sitting on the berthing stands in their own dry dock.

Even so, the British Cabinet would not even release the information, let alone press the case through diplomatic channels. Arms control was still popular in Britain. Also, at the time, the Cabinet hoped they could coax the Italians to go along with the naval limitations that had just been negotiated at the Second London Naval Conference, and they did not want to make British-Italian relations worse than they already were. Eventually the matter was dropped.[14]

Democracy, Public Debate, and Arms Control

One final problem a democracy such as the United States must face in verification is the conflict between free debate and the need to protect intelligence. The free flow of information is the engine of democracy; restrict it and you restrict the ability of politicians to bargain and deliberate, and democracy will be unable to function. Yet arms control requires intelligence for verification, and intelligence requires at least some classification in order to protect its sources of information.

No one has been able to show how to reconcile the protection of intelligence sources and the freedom of expression; the problem is part of the larger question of how to meet the demands of national security while also protecting the civil rights of individuals in a democracy. In theory, we have accepted a compromise: we allow some information to be classified, and then allow relatively small groups of elected officials (such as the members of Congress) to have access to this information.

A democratic government should be able to function and survive this minor restriction on popular rule if all points of view are represented. The problem occurs when restrictions on information distort the debate on arms control and bend public attitudes. In practice, security is never perfect, and so some classified information inevitably leaks out. Since the people leaking the information usually have an ax to grind, this information is almost always leaked selectively, and this can distort the arms control debate.

During the summer of 1985, for example, the vulnerability of American ICBMs to a Soviet attack received attention as the United States prepared its position for the START negotiations. While this issue was being raised, Michael Gordon, then a reporter for the *National Journal*, reported that a recent CIA study concluded that the intelligence community had overestimated the accuracy of the Soviet SS-19 ICBM. The new estimates suggested that, despite earlier assessments to the contrary, the missile was not sufficiently accurate to threaten Minuteman silos. This was important for the arms negotiators, as the number of Soviet ICBM warheads capable of threatening U.S. ICBM silos would be reduced by about half. So it would not be as important to pressure the Soviets for concessions on ICBM deployments, and an arms control settlement could be easier than some hardliners claimed. Gordon has tended to write favorably about arms control and has criticized the Minuteman vulnerability argument, and one can guess why he might want the public to know about the CIA report.

A few months later, though, a leak with a different slant appeared in the *Washington Times,* a newspaper that has generally opposed arms control. The paper reported that U.S. intelligence had discovered that the Soviet Union had been practicing operations of SA-12 antiaircraft missiles with their new SS-25 mobile ICBMs. The Soviets could have merely been trying to find a way to protect their SS-25s from U.S. bombers, which would be an obvious weapon to use against a mobile missile (since a bomber crew could search for a location of the launcher, while a missile could not). On the other hand, the Soviets could have had something else in mind. It was possible that the SA-12s deployed with the SS-25s were actually intended to protect the ICBMs from a *missile* attack, in which case the Soviets would have violated the 1971 ABM Treaty (which banned mobile ABMs and limited each country to one ABM site, which the Soviets built around Moscow). The *Washington Times* was most likely using the leaked information to make a case that the Soviets could not be trusted to obey an arms control agreement.

Selective leaking is a common tactic in politics, but arms control is especially vulnerable. Compared with most subjects, arms control depends more on classified information, if only because of the verification issue. So arms control offers more issues that can be manipulated by leaking. Moreover, the payoff for leaking can be great; arguments based on leaked information are notoriously difficult to rebut without compromising intelligence sources even further.

The problem is really an unfortunate result of the legitimate need to protect secrets in a political system that relies on the free flow of information to function. Intelligence will always be needed to monitor arms control; classification systems will always be necessary to protect intelligence; and the classification of information will always hinder democratic debate on arms control.

• • •

The consequence of the increasing difficulty of strategic arms control could be strained Soviet-American relations. This is ironic, because détente was supposed to be one of the benefits of arms control. The failure of SALT II, for example, was one giant step in a long march away from the détente of the 1970s. And no matter what one thinks of the Soviet Union or of some of the unrealistic expectations of détente, most people would probably agree that "stable" relations between the Soviet Union and the United States would benefit both countries. Yet, given the nature of democratic politics and technology, it seems unlikely that the American system as a whole can support arms control—or at least the kinds of arms control we have concentrated on up to now—over the long haul.

If current weapons present so many problems for verification, why were they ever allowed to be developed? Why wasn't the technology banned? The answer lies in understanding just how technology develops.

CHAPTER FIVE

Can the Technology Be Frozen?
Part One: Who Stops First?

WHY is it so difficult to stop the development of military technology? One reason, of course, is the pork-barrel politics that keep munitions plants producing and military bases operating long after real defense needs are met. Another reason is sheer bureaucratic inertia, in which a weapons lab or military service works on the next generation of weapons simply as a matter of routine. Yet even if these forces were eliminated, governments would still resist freezes on weapon research and development.

Why Countries Do Not Control R & D

Historically, some weapons have been more vulnerable than others to an arms control treaty. Most arms control treaties follow a common pattern of scrapping old weapons, capping current weapons, and leaving research and development uncontrolled.

To understand why, think of what it is like to own a car. Cars, as most of us know all too well, have a limited useful lifetime. The average buyer of a new car probably expects five or six years of use out of it. After that, the car will probably have about 80,000 miles on the odometer, and the owner can look forward to replacing piston rings, bearings, clutches, and performing other repairs that go beyond what most of us would consider "routine maintenance." In the meantime, new models promising better gas mileage and performance will have appeared.

Similarly, when buying a battleship or a missile system, defense officials expect to use it for a certain number of years—more than the five or six years expected of an automobile, but still some fixed amount of time. Sooner or later, the cost of updating and maintaining the weapon system is more than it could possibly be worth; even if the weapon is not completely worn out, the opposition has probably deployed something better, so it would be foolish to sink more money into it. (We could spend hundreds of thousands of dollars modernizing the USS *Constitution,* but the 200-year-old frigate would still be worthless from a military point of view.) Also, old weapons tend to require more maintenance, which costs more as time goes on and spares run out. As a result, old ships, aircraft, and missiles have the least value to the military planner and political leader. This is precisely why they are usually the first casualties of an arms control agreement.

For example, all of the ships scrapped under the Washington Naval Treaty were old ships; the schedule proposed by Hughes, Pratt, Coontz, and Roosevelt worked from the oldest ship in each navy to the newest, stopping when the remaining ships filled the tonnage quota allowed each country. The delegates were willing to go along with this proposal because they knew that most of the ships on the scrapping list were of little military value anyway. Indeed, even before the conference, Britain had already begun scrapping many of the ships eventually designated by the treaty.

Although a battleship built in 1915 did not look much different from a battleship built ten years earlier, the two ships were really in entirely different classes. For one thing, the newer ships were significantly faster. A battleship launched in 1906 typically had a top speed of twenty-one knots; battleships such as the *Queen Elizabeth* (launched in 1915) had a top speed of twenty-five knots. Four knots might not seem like much of a difference, but battleships fought as groups, so the speed of the fleet was determined by the slowest ship in the line. The older ships were just a drag on the operation of the fleet as a whole—which is why Britain was scrapping battleships even before the Washington Conference began.

The older battleships were also rendered useless by the development of long-range gunnery. Before the turn of the century, naval gunnery depended as much on luck as on skill. The basic technology of aiming guns had not changed much for over two hundred years. By World War I, however, a revolution in naval gunnery made all warships constructed earlier obsolete.

Earlier battleships had been fitted with guns of three or four different calibers—four-inch, six-inch, eight-inch, and twelve-inch, for example. Each gun had its own ballistic characteristics. This did not matter much in the 1800s, when the range was just a few hundred yards; the problem came when naval guns acquired ranges of several miles. When a battleship let loose a salvo, it was difficult to tell which splash was made by which gun, and gunners were unable to correct their aim. The HMS *Dreadnought*, considered the first modern battleship because it was the "first all big-gun ship," solved this problem. The *Dreadnought* was significant not because it had big guns, but because they were *all* big. By making all of the guns on the ship the same size, aiming was simplified and the efficiency of each ship was multiplied severalfold. (The U.S. Navy later developed shells that produced a colored cloud when they exploded; each ship had its own color so its gunners knew exactly where their shots were landing.)

The next step was to coordinate the firing of the guns from a central position. The Germans were the first to develop such a system, called "director fire." German gunnery officers used a single telescopic range finder (usually located on top of a mast) and sent instructions to the turrets via a telegraph system. With director fire, if a gunner in, say, Turret A overshot his target and adjusted his aim, the gunner in Turret B could use the information to make his adjustment. This way, the gunners could home in on the correct range more quickly, and once a gunner in one turret scored a hit, the other gunners would know the correct range, too. In later versions, the guns were actually operated from the central control center; the turret crews were responsible just for loading shells and powder. Other navies also adopted this system, so that most battleships launched by the major sea powers after 1914 had director fire.

The advantages of uniform armament, director fire, and other technical innovations were so great that battleships built before these inventions were totally outclassed. So the ships that were discarded under the Washington Treaty were doomed anyway, with or without an arms control agreement.

Similarly, SALT I required the Soviet Union to scrap some of its ICBMs before it could deploy additional submarine-launched missiles. The ICBMs that were scrapped were old SS-7s and SS-8s, which had been deployed in the early 1960s. Not only were these early ICBMs inaccurate, but most were also operated from vulnerable aboveground launching pads rather than silos, making them nearly worthless.

Though countries are willing to scrap old weapons, they are almost never willing to scrap weapons they have just deployed. Just as most people do not sell a new car after only one year (unless it is a lemon), governments are unwilling to scrap current weapons so long as they still have some military usefulness. Pity the politician who must explain to his constituents why the government spent billions of dollars on designing, building, and testing a new weapon only to scrap it just as it enters service.

Whether a country will *stop* building a weapon once it is in production, on the other hand, seems to depend on how much money has already been spent. Countries sometimes agree to limit the production of a weapon, but only if they do not have to write off a significant investment. During the Washington Conference, for example, Charles Evans Hughes proposed freezing naval construction, so that no new ships would be laid down, and ships that were uncompleted would be broken up. All of the countries agreed, except the Japanese, who wanted to finish the *Mutsu* and were absolutely unwilling to budge on the issue, as we saw in Chapter Two.

The Japanese were immovable because of battleship economics. As with most warships, the most visible portion of a battleship—the hull, the superstructure, and the machinery inside—accounted for a small portion of the cost of the ship as a whole. The real costs were in the armor, guns, fire control systems, and navigation systems, which were not added until after the ship was launched. The last third of a battleship might represent two-thirds of its total cost.

In the eyes of the Japanese, the *Mutsu* was not just a ship under construction; it was a completed investment. They claimed it was 98 percent completed (they were exaggerating) and backed their claim by commissioning the ship into their navy.[1] The United States and Great Britain were willing to break up the ships that they had under construction because, even though some of them were technically two-thirds completed, they were in fact less than half paid for.

Likewise, in the SALT negotiations, though the Soviets were willing to scrap the old SS-7s and SS-8s, they have never been willing to scrap their current-generation missiles. Neither has the United States, which has never had to reduce its most capable strategic forces as a result of an arms control treaty.*

But what about research and development?

Generally speaking, countries are completely unwilling to accept restraints on R & D, because expectations for new weapons spring eternal. The faults of a proposed weapon are difficult to know in advance. Weapons do not break or wear out on the drawing board. Proposed weapons do not jam or prove difficult to operate under battlefield conditions. The *virtues* of a yet-to-be-built weapon system, though, are abundantly clear—or at least they will be made clear by the officials, contractors, and whoever else is pushing for its development. Paper bombers easily evade enemy radar; drawing-board space defenses shoot down incoming missiles with remarkable accuracy. The potential payoffs for a military breakthrough are usually so great that government leaders do not like to limit their options.

Another reason why countries are loath to control R & D is that it is extraordinarily difficult to control what is going on in-

---

* Ironically, though any weapons scrapped under arms control will be old, arms control can often *prolong* the life of a weapon that would otherwise be discarded. One example was the Titan II, the large ICBM that the United States deployed in the early 1960s. Though it was inaccurate and dangerous to maintain, it was kept in service because some American officials hoped the Soviets would be willing to trade for it in the SALT II negotiations. Also, most officials probably agreed that it was not a good idea to cut American forces unilaterally while the negotiations were going on. In either case, though the Titans were first deployed in 1962, and were scheduled to be in operation only through the end of the decade, arms control helped to keep them in operation for more than twice as long.

side the heads of scientists and technicians. It is at least theoretically possible to limit hardware to 1054 missiles, 42 submarines, etc. But no treaty can simply stop people from thinking about high-energy particle beams. And as we shall see in the next chapter, it is difficult to define just what is military and what is civilian research and development.

Thus, the most irrelevant weapons (i.e., the oldest) are the easiest to control, and the most threatening weapons (i.e., those planned for the future) are the most difficult. This helps explain some of the sticking points in current strategic arms control negotiations. The Soviet Union has been trying to curb U.S. research in advanced, space-based weapons. The Soviets have even said that they would be willing to trade away about half of their existing offensive missiles—the weapons of the previous decade—in exchange for such a ban. American officials, intent on developing high-tech defensive weapons—presumably the weapons of tomorrow—are unwilling to go along. American officials also know that the Soviet Union has its own research program for laser and particle-beam weapons, and that U.S. intelligence cannot verify a ban on such research.

The Test Ban and the Development of Nuclear Weapons

To see just how difficult it is to control the development of weapon technology, let's look at the effort during the 1950s to ban the testing of nuclear weapons. Why was it so difficult for the United States and the Soviet Union to agree to a nuclear test ban treaty?

Most of the people who have written about the test ban have thought that the main stumbling block was verification—the United States would not trust the Soviets, and the Soviets would not allow a ban to be monitored. But verification was only part of the issue. The controversy was not really over testing nuclear weapons but over developing them.

Testing was necessary for development; though the general principles of how basic atomic weapons work were widely known, the engineering details necessary to build a hydrogen bomb—the logical next step—were not. So testing was necessary to determine the fine points.[2] Neither Soviet nor American officials were willing to accept a test ban while testing was critical to developing a hydrogen bomb. As soon as each country reached the critical point where it had the data necessary to build an effective thermonuclear weapon, it reversed its position on the test ban. In retrospect, the position each country took on the test ban at any given point is not surprising at all.

The first step in a nuclear weapons program is to build a basic atomic bomb. In the simplest terms, nuclear weapons function by releasing the energy binding the protons and neutrons of atomic nuclei. The atoms can be either split apart by fission or forced together by fusion. Either way, the transformation of the nuclei releases energy, much more than can be released by simple chemical reactions like oxidation (e.g., rusting iron) or combustion (e.g., burning coal).

The objective in making a fission device—what is commonly called an atomic bomb—is to assemble a critical mass of fissile material (i.e., a quantity that will spontaneously produce a chain reaction). Fissile materials are heavy elements whose atoms are relatively easy to split. The two elements most often used as fissile materials are U-235, an isotope of uranium, and Pu-239, an isotope of plutonium. Since fissile materials are radioactive, a few atoms are always breaking down into simpler elements, releasing a neutron in the process. In a critical mass, the fissioning of one atom releases a neutron that collides with another atom, fissioning it and releasing yet another neutron, and so on in an uncontrolled chain reaction. The fissioning of each atom releases energy, and the cumulative result is an atomic explosion.

The simplest method of assembling a critical mass is to shoot one subcritical piece of fissile uranium into another inside a gun-barrel device; this technique was used in the Hiroshima bomb. A more efficient (but more complex) method is to surround the fissile material with explosives that compress the fissile material into critical mass. This kind of "implosion device" was used at Alamogordo in the first atomic bomb test and later in the Nagasaki bomb. Implosion devices can use either uranium or plutonium.*

---

* The problem with using plutonium in a gun-type device is that plutonium fissions so quickly the thermal expansion produced by the reaction disassem-

Once tested, a basic fission weapon can be improved through several refinements. One is to surround the core with a reflector that forces neutrons flying out of the exploding weapon back into the core; this enables a greater number of nuclei to fission. Another is to surround the core of the bomb with a tamper, or heavy metal jacket, which will contain the exploding core for a few additional milliseconds, giving more fissile material an opportunity to react before the critical mass disassembles. All of these refinements are relatively simple to make after the basic fission device is proven.

The next steps in improving a fission device require tinkering with the core itself. Different combinations of fissile material can be used to control the speed and extent of the chain reaction, for example. Or "fractional crit" designs can be used to reduce the critical mass required for detonation by compressing the fissile material to higher-than-normal densities. (This is especially important because it reduces the amount of scarce and expensive fissile material needed for each weapon.) Other refinements can be used to reduce the size and weight of the device, giving a designer greater flexibility in packaging a bomb.[3] Taken together, these improvements can raise the yield of a fission weapon from 20 kilotons to 200 kilotons and reduce its size and weight by 80 percent or more.*

---

bles the critical mass before many atoms have an opportunity to fission. Hence, it is necessary to use an implosion device in plutonium bombs in order to contain the critical mass for a sufficient time.

The Manhattan Project developed both a gun-type bomb and an implosion device. Because the technology was so simple and fissile material so scarce, the scientists in the project did not test their first gun-type bomb; it was used on Hiroshima instead. They were less confident the implosion system would work, so they tested the first one they built; this was the device exploded in the Trinity test.

* Most experts estimate the yields of the implosion devices exploded at Alamogordo and Nagasaki at about 22 kilotons; they are less certain of the gun device used at Hiroshima, but estimates range from 12 to 15 kilotons. See Cochran, Arkin, and Hoenig, *Nuclear Weapons Databook*, pp. 31–32.

The theoretical limit of the yield of a pure fission bomb is determined by the critical mass of the fissile material used, assuming that all of the material fissions. The practical limit for a pure fission device is considerably less, and seems to be in the neighborhood of 500 kilotons; see Lapp, *Atoms and People*, p. 101.

Figure 5.1

FISSION WEAPONS

Gun-Type Device

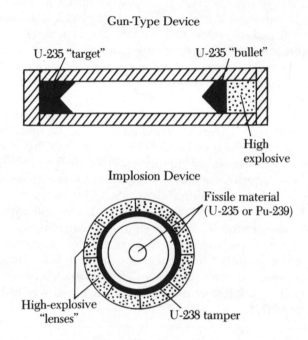

Implosion Device

Once a country's technicians have mastered the technical details of a fission bomb, however, they will very quickly understand how it can be used as the basis of an even more powerful device—a thermonuclear bomb. Fusion is more efficient than fission as a means of producing energy. But fusion is more difficult to achieve because atomic nuclei tend to repel each other, and tremendous pressure and energy are required to overcome this force. Fortunately (or unfortunately, depending on your point of view), an atomic bomb is perfect for providing a large quantity of heat and pressure. The main problem is how to harness it.

The easiest atoms to fuse are light elements. Thermonuclear weapons use either or both of two isotopes of hydrogen—deuterium or tritium. Because these isotopes are gases at room temperatures, though, most weapons substitute a compound called lithium deuteride, which is transformed into hydrogen isotopes in the course of the reaction.

Hydrogen atoms can be fused together simply by putting them into the center of an atomic bomb. This technique is called "boosting," and it is often used to enhance the yield of fission bombs. In boosted weapons a small amount of fusion fuel (either lithium deuteride or tritium gas) is inserted into the center of the weapon. Boosting adds a small thermonuclear explosion to the basic fission explosion; it also releases high-energy neutrons that fission some of the material that would otherwise be scattered by the explosion before it had a chance to react. Boosting can raise the yield of a fission weapon to almost 1,000 kilotons.

However, the space in the core of an atomic bomb is limited, and this limits the amount of hydrogen that can be fused there (and, hence, the size of the explosion). So it is necessary to find some way of fusing hydrogen outside the bomb itself. The invention that makes this possible is called a "Teller-Ulam device," after Edward Teller and Stanislaus Ulam, the physicist and mathematician who originally devised the idea.[4]

In a Teller-Ulam device, energy from a fission bomb trigger is channeled around a mass of hydrogen or lithium deuteride fuel, which is separated by some space from the trigger. (The spacing between the trigger and the fuel is designed to allow the energy to contain the fuel and fuse it before the entire device is destroyed by the exploding trigger.)[5] The energy harnessed from the trigger forces the nuclei of the hydrogen atoms together; an atomic bomb produces energy equivalent to 50,000,000 to 400,000,000 degrees Celsius, or about 10,000 times the temperature of the surface of the sun. The fused hydrogen is transformed into helium, losing a minute amount of matter along the way; this matter, as Einstein predicted, is turned into energy. The reaction also produces high-energy neutrons, which in most thermonuclear weapons are then used to fission a jacket of common uranium U-238 (an isotope of uranium that is ordinarily nonfissile and unsuited for use in a nuclear weapon).

The Teller-Ulam concept is attractive because it provides a way to build a bomb of theoretically infinite size. The size of the explosion is determined primarily by the amount of lithium deuteride and U-238 used, and these compounds, unlike fissile mate-

Figure 5.2

THERMONUCLEAR WEAPON (TELLER-ULAM DEVICE)

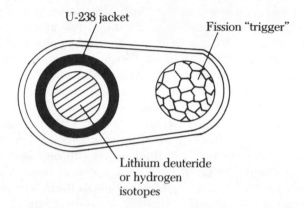

U-238 jacket

Fission "trigger"

Lithium deuteride
or hydrogen
isotopes

rial, are relatively cheap. So, once an atomic weapons program is started, developing a thermonuclear weapon is the most logical endpoint; it makes little sense to stop halfway with "just" a fission weapon. Building an atomic bomb provides the trigger for a hydrogen bomb, and a hydrogen bomb offers the potential of theoretically infinite destructive power at an economical price. The only problems are increasing the efficiency of the fission device so that it emits sufficient energy and working out the details of the Teller-Ulam configuration.

A brief look at the record seems to confirm this. The United States exploded its first atomic bomb in 1945 and tested its first Teller-Ulam device in 1952. The Soviet Union exploded its first atomic bomb in 1949 and tested its first Teller-Ulam device in 1955. Great Britain exploded its first atomic bomb in 1952 and tested its first Teller-Ulam device in 1957. France exploded its first atomic bomb in 1960 and tested its first Teller-Ulam device in 1964. China exploded its first atomic bomb in 1964 and tested its first Teller-Ulam device in 1967. The only exception to this pattern is India, which carried out a "peaceful nuclear explosion" in 1974, and has apparently allowed its military nuclear program to remain stagnant since then.

The American and Soviet Nuclear Programs

For further confirmation of the reluctance of countries to limit promising R & D, let us try to reconstruct the test programs of the United States and the Soviet Union, and then match them to the negotiating record of the two countries.

Within just a few months after V-J Day, most of the Manhattan Project scientists left Los Alamos, leaving it staffed by virtually a skeleton crew. In the early days following the war, the goal of American nuclear policy was to put a lid on the development of nuclear weapons. Harry Truman genuinely feared the spread of the atomic bomb, and even before the war was over he intended to put it under some kind of international control to eliminate the threat. Truman's Secretary of War, Henry Stimson, recommended that the United States, Britain, and the Soviet Union create a "covenant" in which information concerning the peaceful uses of atomic energy could be distributed, but which would also oppose any further military development.[6]

Between September 1945 and the spring of 1946, the United States developed a plan through which the United Nations would control nuclear weapons. The proposal finally developed by Robert Oppenheimer, Dean Acheson, and David Lilienthal would have established an international agency to control the production and distribution of fissile material. The fissile material used for power generation and other peaceful ends would be treated to make it unusable for weapons, which presumably would keep additional countries from acquiring atomic weapons. In return, these countries would be given the opportunity to develop their own peaceful nuclear industries with the technical data that the international agency would distribute freely.

This plan was given to Bernard Baruch, a septuagenarian investor who had been an adviser to presidents for most of the century, to sell to the other members of the UN. The Baruch Plan, as it came to be known, failed because the United States was unwilling to give away the atomic "secret" until the Russians agreed to forgo nuclear weapons and open their country to inspection, while the Soviet Union was unwilling to give up its nuclear weapons program until the Americans put their weapons under international control. As we shall see, the Soviet program was well along by this point.

In the meantime, American nuclear weapon technology lay stagnant. The United States did test two atomic bombs against some obsolete ships in the Bikini atoll in 1946, but these were just demonstrations of atomic bomb effects. The first tests for improving U.S. nuclear weapons—the "Sandstone" series, conducted at Bikini—were put off until 1948. By that time, the Cold War was heating up.

The goal of the Sandstone series was to test the effectiveness of some minor refinements to the original implosion device. Most had been designed and developed during the war, and adding them to the basic Nagasaki-type design posed few problems. As a result of the Sandstone tests, it was possible to increase the yield of the basic bomb to about 50 kilotons, or about twice the yield of the original implosion device.[7]

Then the U.S. nuclear program stagnated again until 1950. The 1948 Berlin Crisis, the first Soviet atomic bomb test in 1949, and the outbreak of the Korean War in 1950 had led the United States to gear itself for competition with the Soviet Union; this policy was codified under NSC 68, and the decision to build advanced nuclear weapons was part of this policy.

The United States conducted more tests, some to improve fission devices, others as part of the hydrogen bomb program. One series, conducted in Nevada, tested the first American fractional crit device and some smaller nuclear weapons designs; these enabled the United States to deploy its first small tactical nuclear weapons.[8] They also improved U.S. technology for the trigger of the hydrogen bomb. Meanwhile, back at the Pacific test range, where the larger devices were exploded, the scientists were preparing another test series, "Greenhouse," which included at least two thermonuclear experiments. One shot, *Item,* appears to have been the first U.S. boosted weapon. Another shot, *George,* was a test to determine whether hydrogen could be fused and the rate at which this reaction occurred—data essential for the design of a Teller-Ulam device.

The *George* device consisted of an atomic bomb into which a mixture of liquefied deuterium and tritium was inserted. The hydrogen isotopes had to be kept liquid so that they would be dense enough to fuse. This required *George* to be equipped with a refrigeration plant, called a "dewer." The scientists knew that *George* had worked when their instrumentation recorded the release of high-energy neutrons in the first millisecond of the explosion—the telltale sign of the fusion reaction.[9]

The task then was to prove that fusion was possible on a larger scale. The proof came at the next set of tests held at the Pacific range, the "Ivy" series, held in the autumn of 1952. The critical test was *Mike,* the first demonstration of a Teller-Ulam device. Like the *George* device, it required a refrigeration plant to keep the deuterium-tritium fuel in liquid form for the reaction. The entire device weighed over 60 tons and occupied a building that resembled a large garage or a small aircraft hangar. *Mike* was successful, yielding a 15-megaton explosion.

The next step was to test a Teller-Ulam device that was a practical weapon. The *Mike* device itself was too big to transport easily (though, in fact, a *Mike*-type device was eventually "weaponized"; it weighed 21 tons). The idea of using lithium deuteride instead of cryogenically liquefied hydrogen isotopes came too late to be used in *Mike*. The first lithium deuteride-fueled Teller-Ulam device—at the time flippantly called a "baking soda bomb"—was tested in the *Bravo* shot of the "Castle" series in 1954. Several variations of the device were tested later in the series.*

As for the Soviet program, a surprising amount of information can be found by reading between the lines of Soviet newspapers and journals. Information can also be gleaned from the memoirs of officials who took part in the program. Some descriptions of Soviet tests can be found in the open press and in official government statements. Using this information, one can deduce

* The *Bravo* test was important for more than just being the first test of a practical U.S. hydrogen bomb. It was also responsible for starting the antinuclear testing movement on a large scale. Up until then, the public probably did not think much about the dangers of fallout. Unfortunately, a Japanese fishing boat, the *Lucky Dragon,* strayed into the restricted area downwind from the test. A sudden shift in the wind brought the radioactive cloud over the trawler. Several of the crewmen became sick, and one later died. This graphic demonstration of the effects of fallout brought many people off the sidelines and put them in favor of banning nuclear tests.

what kind of device the Soviets exploded in most of their early tests.

Herbert York—former director of the Lawrence Livermore Nuclear Laboratory, former Defense Department official, and in recent years one of the leading historians of the nuclear era—reports that even in 1939 the Soviet physicist Igor Tamm told his students that "a bomb could be built that will destroy a city out to a radius of maybe ten kilometers."[10] The Great Purge and the war prevented the Soviets from following through with any real work on an atomic bomb until 1942, when the State Defense Committee (the predecessor of today's Soviet Defense Council) approved a nuclear weapons program, which began under I. V. Kurchatov in February 1943.[11] Kurchatov was to become the Soviet counterpart of Oppenheimer, directing the research for the first Soviet atomic bomb.

Kurchatov had little trouble finding space to house the project. By that time, the Soviets had evacuated much of their industry to the Urals, so there were lots of empty buildings in Moscow, and Kurchatov took over the offices abandoned by the Seismological Institute and Institute for Inorganic Chemistry. As the program grew, Kurchatov expanded into an old artillery range on the outskirts of the city.

The Russian physicists and engineers experimented with atomic bomb designs throughout 1944 and 1945 while they were working on their first reactor. When the United States succeeded in exploding the first nuclear weapon at Alamogordo, the Soviet program was accelerated. According to I. N. Golovin, Kurchatov's biographer and colleague, it was then that "the Government of the USSR called upon Soviet scientists and engineers to make an atomic bomb of their own in the shortest possible time."[12]

From Golovin's account, it seems that the Soviets followed a path similar to that of the Manhattan Project. The first task was to obtain sufficient fissile uranium for a nuclear reactor; this reactor was then used to produce plutonium, which was then used as weapon material. The first Soviet reactor "went critical" in December 1946. (Golovin's description of how the first Soviet reactor was built sounds remarkably like the account of Enrico

Fermi's team assembling the first atomic pile under the bleachers at the University of Chicago football stadium.)

The Soviets later built a permanent reactor for producing plutonium. The first minute amounts of plutonium were given to the chemists and metallurgists so that they could figure out how to shape it into components for the bomb. Finally, in August 1949, the Soviets tested their first nuclear device—most likely a device similar to the American one tested at Alamogordo and used at Nagasaki—near Semipalatinsk, in the southern USSR. Like Los Alamos, Semipalatinsk is still used as a nuclear development center.

This Soviet test—called "Joe 1" in the West, after Joseph Stalin—was announced by the United States, which had set up a worldwide detection network just a few months before. Airplanes flying just off the northern and eastern coasts of the Soviet Union collected air samples and tested the atmosphere for radioactive fallout from a test explosion. In late August they found traces of radiation on photographic plates and the chemical residue of a plutonium chain reaction in the air samples. (The latter was the tip-off that the Soviets had developed an implosion device.)

The Soviets appear to have had enough fissile material on hand for a backup device. According to Golovin, Kurchatov worried that the first bomb might be a dud and demoralize the members of the project—not to mention the government and military officials, who Golovin says were present at the first test. There is no evidence that this second bomb was detonated; most likely, once Joe 1 was successful, the Soviets decided to conserve their fissile material. In any case, they do not appear to have exploded another nuclear weapon until two years later, in October 1951, when the United States detected the fallout from another test. (We do not know if they attempted more tests than this; Soviet "fizzles" were difficult to detect at the time because the United States had little reconnaissance of Soviet territory.)

The first test in the 1951 series was described by Senator Edwin Johnson, a member of Congress's Joint Atomic Energy Committee, as having also used plutonium and having a yield equal to that of the Nagasaki bomb, about 20 kilotons.[13] Presumably Senator Johnson had information provided by the U.S. Atomic Energy

Commission, which his committee was responsible for supervising. The reports that appeared in the Soviet press at the time suggest that the 1951 detonations, Joe 2 and Joe 3, were most likely tests of the first Soviet fission devices using higher-efficiency or miniaturized designs. Two days after Senator Johnson made his statement to the American press, Stalin said in a *Pravda* interview, "It is true that we recently tested one type of atomic bomb. Atom bombs *of various calibers* will continue to be tested in the future in accordance with the plan for the defense of our country against an attack by the Anglo-American aggressive bloc."[14] Similarly, in an article published five months later in the Soviet military press, Major General Petr Korkodinov wrote that "to meet the enemy fully armed [the Soviet government] has organized the production and testing of atomic bombs of various calibers."[15] It is unclear whether "calibers" referred to size or explosive yield, but in either case it is apparent that the Soviets were improving upon the simple implosion device used in the first test.

The next Soviet tests were held in 1953. In his August 8 address to the Supreme Soviet (the titular parliament of the Soviet Union), then-Premier Georgy Malenkov referred to the American *Mike* shot conducted the preceding November: just as "the United States has no monopoly on the atomic bomb, it has no monopoly on the hydrogen bomb, either." Four days later, the Soviets exploded a nuclear device, Joe 4.

American analysts discovered that the fallout from the Soviet test contained traces of lithium deuteride. At first, this was taken to mean that the Soviets had developed a Teller-Ulam device—that is, a device like the one the United States had tested during Operation Ivy in the *Mike* shot; this was understandable, considering Malenkov's statement before the test. More troubling, though, was the fact that the lithium deuteride residue from the Soviet test suggested that their bomb was portable; the *Mike* device that the United States had tested the preceding year was not.

More recently, though, Herbert York has deduced that the 1953 Soviet device was in all likelihood not a Teller-Ulam device after all. Golovin described the test in his biography of Kurchatov.[16] The bomb, which was suspended from a tower, "vaporized" the tower and its foundation, created a "huge crater," and converted the surrounding soil into a "caked, glassy, yellow mass, striated with cracks and covered with fused lumps." This might seem impressive, but when *Mike* was exploded, Eugalab, the islet that the device was built upon, vanished completely and was replaced by a half-mile-deep crater. Apparently the Soviet test was much less powerful than the American test. York, who was at the *Mike* test, estimates that the effects of the Soviet test on the tower and surrounding earth imply a weapon that had less than a megaton yield—probably not more than 500 kilotons. This was significantly less than one would expect from a first trial of a Teller-Ulam device.[17]

Most likely Joe 4 was a test of the booster principle, the same kind of device that the United States tested in the *Item* and *George* shots during Operation Greenhouse in 1951. This would make sense, as the Soviets would have needed data on thermonuclear reactions before they could make the calculations necessary for designing a Teller-Ulam device.

Following Joe 4, the Soviets carried out several more tests, some using various kinds of pure fission bombs, others using boosted weapons.[18] During this period they were also studying the effects of nuclear weapons on military equipment and civilian structures—just as the United States did in its first dozen or so tests. According to Soviet accounts, even in the Joe 1 test, the Soviets located a number of tanks and guns near the explosion to observe the effects.[19] According to Golovin, the Joe 4 explosion tipped over a locomotive and knocked down test walls that had been built nearby.[20] The reports in the Soviet press at the time suggest that the tests conducted around 1954 were similar to those that the United States had carried out at the Nevada test range beginning in 1951. Like the Americans, the Soviets probably had some civil defense plans in mind; in a TASS communiqué issued September 17, 1954, for example, the Soviet government announced:

> In accordance with the plan for scientific research, a test of one of the types of atomic weapons has been carried out in the Soviet Union in recent days. The object of the test was to study the action of an atomic explosion. During the test valuable results were obtained which will help Soviet scientists and engineers to solve the problems of success against atomic attack.[21]

Some of these tests were probably also connected with military exercises, to train Soviet troops to fight, as the expression goes, "in a nuclear environment." The United States had already carried out similar tests in Nevada (Operation Smokey and the Army's Desert Rock exercises). The object was to simulate what it would be like to go on the offensive behind a nuclear artillery barrage. The Army took regular combat troops to the range, where they would dig in close to ground zero. Some officers who had volunteered for a ringside seat were as close as a half-mile from the explosion. After the device was exploded, the soldiers would climb out of their foxholes and advance toward ground zero. (Some later filed suit against the government, claiming they had contracted cancer from the exposure to radiation.)

What the Soviets were up to at this time is suggested by an account written ten years later by Major General S. N. Kozlov, who recalled:

> Beginning in 1954, all combat training in the Soviet Armed Forces began to be conducted with a calculation of using the atomic weapon. From that time on Soviet military thought began urgently to work out new problems of conducting armed combat connected with the development of the nuclear rocket weapon.[22]

The next major step in Soviet nuclear weapons development did not occur until November 1955. At that time the Soviets detonated a very large nuclear device, yielding an explosion of at least one megaton. Nikita Khrushchev happened to be traveling in India at the time, and described the device to reporters:

> The tests have demonstrated important new achievements by our scientists and engineers. The latest explosion of an H-bomb has been the most powerful to this time. Using a relatively small quantity of fissionable material, our scientists and engineers have managed to produce an explosion equal to several megatons of conventional explosives.[23]

This was probably the first test of the Soviet Teller-Ulam device. The date was to be important in the diplomatic maneuvering over the test ban.

Other countries seem to have followed the same path in developing a practical thermonuclear capability. This makes sense; after all, the laws of physics in New Mexico are approximately the same as those in the Sinkiang Province of China. A chronological summary of the first six Chinese nuclear tests is revealing:[24]

Test No.	Date	Yield	Remarks
1	Oct. 16, 1964	20 kt.	Conducted from tower, uranium device
2	May 15, 1965	20–40 kt.	Conducted from tower, probably plutonium device
3	May 9, 1966	200 kt.	Conducted at 10,000-foot altitude
4	Oct. 26, 1966	20–40 kt.	Ballistic missile shot
5	Dec. 29, 1966	300 kt.	Contained lithium
6	June 17, 1967	3 mt.	Atmospheric shot

It would seem that Test #1 was a basic fission weapon; this may have been a Hiroshima-style gun device, as it used uranium. Test #2 was possibly the first Chinese implosion device, as it was definitely the first Chinese plutonium bomb—the Chinese version of Operation Trinity or Joe 1. Test #3 probably introduced the usual measures for increasing the efficiency of a fission bomb—improved tampers, reflectors, etc.—and would have been the Chinese version of Operation Sandstone. Test #4 may have been of a lightweight warhead (one that could be carried by a missile), or perhaps it was simply a test of a complete nuclear weapon system. Test #5 was probably the first Chinese bomb using the booster principle, like *Item, George,* or *Joe 4.* The sixth Chinese test was their first Teller-Ulam device.

The British and French followed similar paths. The American and Soviet programs differ from the British, French, and Chinese mainly in the greater number of tests the superpowers carried out between each technological step; the United States and the Soviet Union are wealthier and could afford to test more. Also, modern computers have made it easier for the more recent nuclear powers to derive more data from each explosion.

Testing and the Test Ban

The similarity in these test programs is interesting, but what the programs suggest about the feasibility of a test ban is more important. For example, the Soviet Union resolutely opposed a test ban for years. Even after Stalin had died, Soviet leaders held fast: no test ban until after the United States agreed to give up its nuclear weapons. This line continued through 1954 and most of 1955. Then, in May 1955, the Soviets abruptly changed their position and proposed a total ban on nuclear weapons tests, to take effect the following January.[25]

The timing of their proposal is significant. Remember, the first Soviet Teller-Ulam bomb was tested in November 1955—*two months before the test ban that the Soviets proposed would have gone into effect.* A nuclear test requires months of preparation, so it is safe to conclude that the Soviet scientists were assembling their first Teller-Ulam device even as the Soviet political leaders were proposing to ban further tests the following year. In other words, the Soviets wanted first to prove their Teller-Ulam device, and then shut the door on any other countries hoping to build a similar weapon.

Figure 5.3

SELECTED NUCLEAR TESTS AND PROPOSALS FOR TEST BANS

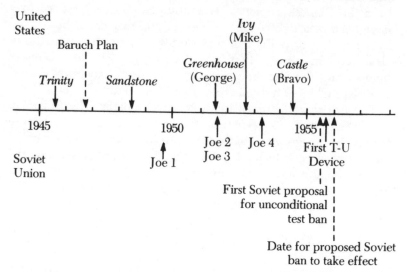

After the Soviets accepted the principle of a test ban, the two superpowers jockeyed for position. The tests they carried out after 1956 were aimed at either perfecting warheads tailored for specific weapon systems, or simply acquiring more information about thermonuclear explosions. Neither American nor Soviet leaders wanted to give their opponent the last move in weapons development before tests were prohibited.

The Soviets tested a record number of nuclear weapons through 1957. They accelerated their test program even more in the first three months of 1958, sometimes exploding two devices on a single day. Then, in March 1958, the Soviet government announced that it would cease its test program unilaterally, and would not resume, provided other countries also ceased.

The United States was still reluctant to accept a complete ban on testing. As always, the problem of verifying Soviet compliance remained. However, after conducting a final test series (Operation Hardtack II, in which thirty-seven weapons were detonated in forty-eight days), the United States accepted the Soviet offer. The Soviets resumed testing, too, and finally stopped after the major powers agreed to meet at Geneva in order to negotiate a long-term treaty banning nuclear testing.

The moratorium on nuclear tests held until September 1961. By then, the nuclear powers had negotiated for three years for a permanent test ban. The sticking point was finding a means of verification that would satisfy both American worries over Soviet violations and also the Soviet penchant for secrecy. The Soviets broke the moratorium first, testing even more weapons than they had in 1957. The United States responded the following year.

Eventually the test ban dispute was settled by not banning tests at all. Rather, the superpowers agreed in 1963 to test only underground, in order to reduce the danger of fallout. This Partial Test Ban Treaty did reduce the fallout problem, and people no longer talk about how much strontium 90 their milk contains. However, the Partial Test Ban had little effect on the development of nuclear weapons. By the time it was adopted, the United States and the Soviet Union had ample information about the aboveground effects of nuclear explosions. Both countries were beginning to reduce the average yield of their weapons (small weapons can be tested more easily underground), and by 1963 nuclear weapon technology had become sufficiently mature that it was no longer necessary to conduct full-scale tests of 10-megaton operational warheads in any case.

Oddly enough, the Partial Test Ban may have even contributed to the further development of nuclear weapons. To obtain the support of the military and the nuclear weapons industry, President Kennedy promised, in submitting the treaty for Senate approval, that the United States would embark on an expanded test program. The result was the development of the small nuclear devices eventually used in MIRVs, cruise missiles, and other modern strategic weapons systems. The lesson of the struggle for a nuclear test ban is that it is extraordinarily difficult, if not impossible, to defeat the incentives that drive countries to develop new military technology. If the "sweetness" of the technology does not lure a country forward, the threat—real or not—of a military imbalance will.

The question is always what comes next. Even now, for example, it is apparent that there are ways to take nuclear weapons the next step beyond a Teller-Ulam device. One objective could be to use a nuclear weapon to supply energy for a laser; instead of using the energy from a fission bomb trigger to fuse hydrogen nuclei, as in a Teller-Ulam device, this "nuclear-pumped" laser would focus the energy of the weapon into a directed X-ray beam for a microsecond before the apparatus was obliterated by the explosion. The beam could then be used, say, to destroy missiles in flight.

U.S. scientists are aware of these possibilities; such devices are under study in the Reagan Administration's Strategic Defense Initiative. Moreover, the Department of Defense has reported that the Soviet Union is working on directed-energy weapons, too.[26] As in the past, neither side is willing to sign away its prerogative to develop these weapons.* If the past is any guide,

---

* The Soviet Union has pressed the United States for a treaty banning space-based defensive weapons; for example, at the Reykjavik Summit, Gorbachev proposed an extension of the 1972 ABM Treaty. Gorbachev also proposed modifying the treaty so that it would more clearly prohibit the testing of space-based weapons such as those the United States is developing. How-

both sides will probably insist on protecting these future weapons, and the technology will be developed.

Yet, there is still another question to ask: What causes the technology to press forward in the first place? Why can't military technology simply be halted? The answer is, as we shall see next, in the nature of technology itself.

---

ever, the proposal apparently would not inhibit the *Soviet* programs now under way. The defensive directed-energy weapons the Soviets are developing are, according to published reports, based on earth, and ground-based weapons are not mentioned in the Soviet proposals. Indeed, the Soviets do not even acknowledge that their directed-energy weapons program exists.

CHAPTER SIX

Can the Technology Be Frozen?
Part Two: The Technological Web

WHY *is* it so difficult to stop the development of military technology?

The question begins with a misconception; there is really no such thing as "military technology" per se. Some technology is especially useful for waging war, but military technology consists of ideas and applications that are woven into the fabric of society. Military technology cannot be eliminated without radically altering society itself.

For example, suppose that someone wanted to eliminate or control "automobile technology." To do so, one would have to restrict the development of basic concepts such as pneumatic tires, internal combustion engines, and transmissions. If one were *really* serious, one would want to "disinvent" the wheel and erase knowledge of carbon chemistry and ferrous metallurgy.

Of course, this would be as impossible as it is undesirable. First, almost all of the technologies associated with automobiles have other applications; wheels are used in trains, internal combustion engines are used in airplanes, and so on. Unless one were also willing to restrict trains, planes, and other common conveniences, the technology necessary to make an automobile would be reinvented very quickly and we would be back where we started.

Second, and possibly even more important, the development of technology is largely unpredictable. Take the automobile engine, for example. Nicolaus Otto, the German engineer who patented the first internal combustion engine, was not thinking of automobiles when he invented the four-stroke gasoline engine in 1876; rather, he was trying to design a power plant for industrial applications, such as driving cloth looms or powering hydraulic pumps. To have prevented the development of automobile technology, one would have had to predict the complex, interconnected chain of events that would lead to its invention. The problem that prevents us from capping technology, military or otherwise, is that there are probably a hundred or more different ways in which one idea can lead to another, and knowing all of these possible connections in advance is impossible.

Consider the tank. According to folklore, a small group of British engineers invented the tank as a secret weapon in World War I. The German attack on the Western Front had stalled in 1914, and the combatants found themselves stuck in miles upon miles of muddy trenches. Nothing, it seemed, would enable one side to dislodge the other. Finally, the story goes, the British designed a revolutionary war machine that could crawl through the trenches even under machine-gun fire and artillery. Sometimes it is said that the British could have won the war in 1916 if only they had been more daring with their tanks.

In truth, the development of the tank is a much more complex story that illustrates how complicated controlling military technology can be.

The idea of an armored vehicle is ancient. Hannibal's elephants were a form of armored assault vehicle, and Leonardo da Vinci was designing tanks as early as 1488. The main problem was not coming up with the *idea* of the tank, but developing the various components and bringing them together. Some of these components are obvious, e.g., caterpillar tracks (invented in 1770 in Britain by R. L. Edgeworth).[1] Some of the obstacles are less obvious because it was not so much that a component was missing as it was that the necessary technology was immature. For instance, because the inventions of steel and internal combustion engines were so new in 1890, a bulletproof tank built at that time would have been so overweight and underpowered that it would not have been able to move.[2]

The important point to understand is that most of the breakthroughs that eventually made the tank possible were not originally developed for it. Edgeworth was not interested in war machines; he designed his caterpillar drive system for farm tractors. Similarly, high-tensile steel was used in bridges long before it was used to armor vehicles.

In fact, almost all of the technology necessary for the tank was lying around at the time the British were searching for a trench-crossing vehicle. The only question was who would assemble it all into a tank. As one might expect, at least four different countries were developing tanks in 1915, all apparently unaware of each other's efforts. Indeed, there were two separate teams designing tanks in Britain alone—one in the Ministry of War, the other in the Admiralty—and they worked for at least a year before discovering each other's existence.

In order to prevent British engineers from conjuring up the idea of a tank, one would have had to have interfered with the ideas of internal combustion engines, armor, and Caterpillar tractors, and to have stopped everyone interested in building a tank—after finding out who and where they were. This we are unable or unwilling to do. The development of military technology is so complex that it probably cannot be predicted, let alone controlled.

It is clear from past arms control negotiations that the technological web is not just a sociological abstraction. It is a real problem, and when negotiations bump up against it, they stop. This is what happened when Charles Evans Hughes attempted to control the development of strategic bombers.

By the early 1920's, people could see the promise (or horror) that strategic bombers presented. Aviation technology was just reaching the point at which it was possible to build an airplane capable of carrying a significant bomb load to targets hundreds of miles away, and fast enough to evade enemy fighters and flak. A few primitive bombers had even been used in World War I, hinting at the weapons of future wars, much as the "smart bombs" used in the last years of the Vietnam War hinted at the precision-guided munitions of today.

By the twenties people began to regard bombers as a serious threat. Descriptions of this threat would sound familiar to anyone reading about the threat of high-energy particle beams or antisatellite weapons. Writers in the 1920s began spinning tales about how countries would bomb each other's cities, creating wholesale slaughter (a threat that was realized in World War II) and perhaps using poison gas (one threat that was not).

The popular fear of strategic bombing made bombers a serious issue in the early stages of the Washington Conference. (Although the Washington Conference is usually identified with naval limitations, the meeting in fact was scheduled to discuss all kinds of weapons.) Yet, though Hughes was sympathetic to the idea of limiting bombers, he encouraged his colleagues to skip over the issue. He realized that the difficulty of controlling bombers could have put the entire conference off track.

Hughes understood that "bomber technology" is as amorphous as "military technology" is in general. Bombers are not especially different from other kinds of aircraft; they fly lower and faster than passenger airplanes of the same size, but the technology is basically the same. Indeed, the similarity would surprise most people. The B-1B bomber, for example, draws heavily on the data generated for the stillborn American supersonic transport (SST) of the late 1960s and early 1970s. The fanjet engines for the B-1B borrow from the technology developed for airliners in reaction to the fuel crisis of the 1970s.*

The main difference between bombers and airliners in the 1920s was whether the doors were on the side (for people and cargo) or on the bottom (for a bomb bay). So the other negotiators quickly agreed with Hughes that trying to ban bombers would be fruitless. In the quaint words of the conference report, bombers could not be banned because doing so would "limit a technology that promises to be a boon to civilization."

In the current Soviet-American arms control negotiations, one of the key sticking points is "ASAT," antisatellite weapons. Arms control advocates fear that ASATs could be used to destroy an opponent's early-warning satellites, which are used to detect the exhaust plumes of ICBMs breaking through the atmosphere. Attacking early-warning satellites makes sense from a military

---

* The technological flow operates in the other direction, too; the modern, high-precision inertial guidance systems used in modern oceanic airliners were originally developed for military aircraft and missiles.

standpoint, since one does not want to give the enemy any warning, much less early warning. ASAT opponents fear that with their early-warning systems destroyed, the Soviet Union and the United States would be like two blind giants slugging at each other in the dark with nuclear weapons—not exactly a comforting prospect. So arms control advocates support an ASAT ban. If, they say, the two superpowers could just agree to avoid testing ASAT systems now, before they are operational, the next level in the arms race could be avoided. But is this true?

Most attention in the ASAT debate has focused on two weapons specifically designed to destroy satellites. One is the "coorbital interceptor" deployed by the Soviet Union. It is essentially a satellite that makes only one or two orbits and is designed to destroy another satellite. It is based on a modified SS-9 ICBM which is used to place an interceptor device into an orbit that intersects with that of the satellite targeted for destruction. As the warhead approaches the satellite, it explodes like a shotgun shell, spraying shrapnel into the target. By 1985, the Soviets had tested their ASAT against practice targets about a dozen times, destroying them about half the time.

The other ASAT that was the focus of controversy in 1985 was the American ASAT, cobbled together by mounting a SRAM (an air-to-ground "short-range attack missile" usually used on U.S. bombers) onto an F-15 fighter. The "warhead" is a small cylinder officially referred to as a "maneuvering vehicle" or "MV," though some technicians have nicknamed it the "tomato can" (which it resembles, assuming one buys canned tomatoes in the large economy size). It is equipped with tracking telescopes and guidance rockets. In an antisatellite mission, the F-15 would fly to high altitude and fire the ASAT, which would then home in on the target with tremendous speed. The tomato can is supposed to be so accurate that it will destroy a satellite by its sheer impact; it carries no explosive charge.[3]

Almost everyone thought that the American ASAT was potentially a much more useful—and destabilizing—weapon than the Soviet ASAT. The Soviet weapon required a large launching pad, while the American ASAT could be based wherever there was enough room for an F-15 to take off. Monitoring a limit on the number of Soviet-style ASATs would be essentially the same problem as limiting SS-9s, as in SALT I. The MV, however, could be launched from any appropriately modified F-15, so it would be impossible to monitor it without keeping track of every F-15.

Arms control advocates tried hard to stop the testing of the American ASAT. Walter Mondale, for example, campaigned in 1984 in part on the slogan "Draw the Line in the Skies," meaning that he would oppose the development of space weapons such as ASATs. ASAT opponents feared that if the United States proved that its system worked, the Soviets would respond by building their own "tomato can." Hence, an ASAT treaty soon became the arms control topic of the day, but in the end, neither the Soviet nor the American system was curbed.

Yet ASAT opponents might have been missing the development of an even more ominous system. Even while the anti-ASAT campaign was being waged full-bore, the United States was testing a real, functional antisatellite system in space and broadcasting the exercise on live television.

This ASAT was pictured on the cover of *Aviation Week* for November 16, 1984. The picture was taken during a mission of the space shuttle *Discovery*, and shows American astronauts Dale Gardner and Joseph Allen wrestling with the Weststar 6 satellite while orbiting in space. The Weststar had fallen into a low, irregular orbit when its booster rocket failed during deployment on an earlier shuttle mission. In the photograph, Gardner, wearing a spacepack that enables him to maneuver in space, is grabbing one end of the satellite; Allen, his feet anchored to the manipulator arm of the shuttle, is holding the other end. Eventually the two astronauts got the satellite into the shuttle's cargo bay, strapped it down, and carried it back to earth, where it was refurbished and prepared for a second launch attempt.

So there already exists a simple, effective, and—possibly most important—proven American ASAT: an astronaut standing on the manipulator arm of the space shuttle, grabbing a satellite out of orbit. Few reporters in the American press said much about the possibility that the shuttle could perform this same mission against a *Soviet* satellite. The Soviet press did, though. Indeed, Soviet journalists usually portray the U.S. shuttle program as mainly military. When the shuttle *Challenger* tragically exploded during liftoff in January 1986, the Soviet press communicated its regrets for the crew, but cast them as victims of a Defense Department that had forced NASA to develop the shuttle too fast. Of course, the Soviet press has said nothing about its own space shuttle, which appears to be a clone of the U.S. spacecraft and will most likely be capable of satellite-scooping missions, too.[4]

To be sure, the current shuttle would not be a highly effective antisatellite weapon; it flies too low to capture most Soviet military satellites. But as long as a shuttle can maneuver to within a few hundred yards of a satellite, it can probably put it out of action, and eventually shuttles will become more advanced, more maneuverable, and higher-flying. At some point they will be easily convertible into satellite-killers.

Can there be an effective ASAT treaty without banning space shuttles? We probably cannot restrict them without "depriving civilization of a great boon," any more than the Washington negotiators could ban bombers without hamstringing civilian aviation in the process. Space shuttles offer too many potential benefits to too many people. As they inevitably become more and more advanced, any legalisms preventing them from being configured as antisatellite weapons will become more and more fragile.

What would happen if an ASAT ban were signed? The development of purely military ASATs, such as the Soviet co-orbital system and the American MV, would stop. However, space shuttles would continue to be developed. As they improved, people would realize that the treaty was a sham; converting a civilian shuttle into a satellite interceptor would be too easy. Probably the United States and the Soviet Union would frequently accuse each other of trying to circumvent the treaty.

And what if one side or the other *did* decide to quit the treaty? The technology necessary to build a full-fledged ASAT would be easier to perfect as civilian shuttles were developed further. It would be easier for a country to *suddenly* deploy its ASAT before its opponent could respond. In arms control parlance, this threat is called "breakout potential." In other words, an ASAT treaty would lead to a more precarious state of affairs.*

---

* Some arms control supporters argue that there are "critical periods" in the

Anticipating the Technological Web

With the conservative turn American politics has taken, many people believe that free markets work better than planned economies; they argue that hordes of independent thinkers are more creative than centralized planners. It is ironic, then, that many of the same people also believe that an arms control planner can outwit the hordes of inventors developing ideas for new weapons.

The entangling web of technology makes it incredibly difficult to predict the chain of events that will lead to the development of a particular new weapon. Who would have thought that the Jacquard loom would lead to the design of computers, which led to the development of high-accuracy inertial guidance systems, which in turn have made it possible to build an ICBM with a nine-out-of-ten chance of putting a warhead into a 200-yard circle halfway around the world?

Even when the technology seems "purely military," predicting what will lead to what can be extraordinarily difficult. As we have seen, strategic weapons of all kinds—ICBMs, cruise missiles, bombers—have been steadily becoming smaller and lighter. Why is this so? One reason is that the engines in the weapons of today are two to three times more efficient than those in the weapons at the beginning of the nuclear era. The jet engine in the GLCM, for example, is about twice as efficient pound-for-pound as the engine in the first American cruise missile in 1948. A second reason for the shrinkage in strategic weapons is the

---

testing of a weapon and that, if development were halted before this stage were reached, the weapon could be banned. For example, limiting ICBM tests, they say, would block deployment of a new ICBM because no one could be confident that a never-tested ICBM would work.

This argument might be valid in the short run, but not in the long run. Over time, technology that is at first used only in weapons eventually becomes common in society as a whole. In the early days of gas warfare, for example, highly specialized facilities were required to manufacture poison gas, while today almost any pesticide plant has the capability. Or to give another example, as inertial guidance systems become cheaper and more common in commercial aircraft, they could be readily adapted for military use. In either case, one can see that eventually the leap from civilian to military use becomes easier and easier. So, at some point, a ban on testing does little to reduce the confidence that some kind of weapon will work.

improvements made in guidance systems; as weapons become more accurate, they require a smaller explosive charge to produce the same destructive effect, so the entire weapon can be made smaller. A third reason is the advances made in the lightweight plastics and metals that are used in the airframes of these weapons.

These technologies all have strong roots in the civilian sector, and one could not have expected an arms control treaty to have limited their development. High-efficiency jet engines, for example, would most likely have been built in response to the energy crises of the 1970s, no matter what the military had done.

Of course, not every component in a weapon system has its civilian counterpart. Could the development of weapons be limited by limiting development of these critical military components? Probably not; military technology is not planned any more thoroughly than civilian technology, so defense programs can often have unanticipated results that undermine arms control. For example, strategic weapons are smaller today not only because there are better engines and airframes, but also because nuclear warheads are much more efficient. The earliest nuclear weapons, such as the "Little Boy" dropped on Hiroshima and the "Fat Man" dropped on Nagasaki, weighed 8,000–10,000 pounds each. Even into the early 1950s, U.S. nuclear weapons were essentially assembly-line versions of these cumbersome devices. And the first American thermonuclear device—the Mk-17 bomb deployed in the mid-1950s—weighed 43,000 pounds.

Nowadays nuclear weapons are much, much smaller. Some of the smallest devices, such as nuclear land mines (known as atomic demolition munitions, or ADMs), weigh only about 150 pounds and can even be carried in a backpack. (ADMs are designed to destroy bridges, tunnels, and other targets that a commando squad might assault.) The nuclear warheads designed for strategic weapons are not much bigger; the warheads carried on a submarine-launched missile such as the Trident, for example, look like the traffic cones found near a highway construction project and weigh only about 250 pounds. In large part, it is the 250-pound warhead that makes it possible to construct a 32,000-pound ICBM, and it is such small ICBMs that make it possible to deploy a land-based strategic missile force almost anywhere.

Yet even though nuclear warhead design is a purely military technology, the paths that led to miniaturized strategic warheads would still have been difficult to predict. In the early days of the nuclear age, no one thought much about how small nuclear weapons would affect either strategic deterrence or arms control. Indeed, the service most responsible for U.S. strategic forces— the Air Force—*opposed* miniaturization. During the years following World War II, the Air Force had sole authority to deploy nuclear weapons and fought hard to protect its turf. Air Force generals such as Curtis LeMay and Thomas Powers argued that U.S. forces for strategic nuclear bombing were the only means the United States had to deter the Soviet Union and its powerful conventional forces. The Air Force also argued that fissile materials were too scarce and too precious to be diverted to any other use (i.e., the smaller weapons the Army and the Navy might use). In the early days of the nuclear era, the competition between the Air Force and the other services for control over nuclear weapons was so fierce that the Navy had difficulty obtaining even the external dimensions of the weapons in order to design an airplane capable of carrying them.

The main reason the Air Force monopoly was broken in the early 1950s was the formation of NATO. NATO members realized almost immediately that their alliance could not match the conventional forces of the Soviet Union and its allies. The Air Force solution to this problem was to plan to destroy Soviet fuel depots and transportation centers in strategic bombing missions. Unfortunately, studies carried out at the time suggested that Soviet forces would still be able to keep rolling to the English Channel. Hence, something had to be done about the Soviet forces themselves.

The solution pushed by the Eisenhower Administration turned out to be "tactical" nuclear weapons that could be fired directly at the Soviet divisions. These took the form of nuclear artillery shells and nuclear-armed short-range missiles, to be used much as their conventional counterparts had been used for decades: find the enemy unit, give its coordinates to the artillery units, and then bombard the designated location. The difference, of course, was that a few nuclear artillery shells could produce the same destruction as an entire division's artillery over several hours against the same target. Since the Army could not use the first-generation atomic warheads, which weighed four to five tons apiece, the answer was smaller warheads.

The first tactical nuclear device was the Mk-5 bomb, which weighed just over 2,000 pounds. The Mk-5 would have been used by fighter aircraft in ground support missions and was the warhead for the Matador, the first nuclear-armed guided missile. Even smaller atomic devices soon followed, such as the artillery shell designed for the Army's 280-millimeter howitzer. (Known in the press as the "Atomic Cannon," this gun had been designed in World War II and was essentially an updated version of the siege cannons that had been used in World War I.) The gun was portable, though just barely; it was designed to be suspended between two tractor units so that its weight would be distributed over a wider area, enabling the contraption to be transported on the rickety bridges found throughout the European countryside.

The Mk-9 shell was a simple atomic device by today's standards, but it was still a remarkable improvement over the weapons of just five years before, weighing only about 500 pounds. As tactical warheads were further refined, yield-to-weight ratios improved, and it became possible to build smaller weapons without sacrificing much destructive power. Since tactical and strategic warheads are often designed by the same people, when a new technique was developed to build a smaller, more efficient tactical weapon, the new technology was naturally used in the next generation of strategic weapons.

Yet it is important to understand that this trend toward miniaturized nuclear devices would have come as a great surprise to most of the early bomb designers. Consider, for instance, Bernard Brodie, possibly the first strategic nuclear analyst. Brodie, who wrote his first book about the strategic and political implications of nuclear weapons less than a year after Hiroshima, is responsible for much of our thinking about nuclear weapons today. (For example, Brodie seems to have been the first to point out that deterring a nuclear attack is usually more important than defending against one, since even small leaks in a defense would be unbelievably costly.) Though Brodie was prescient on many issues, even he did not anticipate how small nuclear weapons would become; he thought that nuclear weapons would always be huge. Brodie wrote:

> It is clear that the engine necessary for utilizing the explosive, that is, the bomb itself, is a highly intricate and fairly massive mechanism. The massiveness is not something we can expect future research to diminish. It is inherent in the bomb. . . . A little reflection will indicate that the mechanism which can accomplish this must be ingenious and elaborate in the extreme, and certainly not one which can be slipped into a suitcase.[5]

Just twenty years later, the Army designed exactly that: the W54 Special Atomic Demolition Munition, for use by special forces units. The W54 weighs about 150 pounds and is carried in a duffel bag.[6]

Similarly, when the decision to build the first American thermonuclear weapon was being debated, almost everyone thought the hydrogen bomb would inevitably be big: Robert Oppenheimer wrote in 1953 that it would "require an oxcart" to get it to its target (this is one reason why Oppenheimer believed the bomb was impractical).[7] Recalling the size of the original *Mike* device, one can understand this misapprehension. Oppenheimer would be surprised today to see the W-80, a thermonuclear warhead used in cruise missiles, which weighs a mere 270 pounds.

Few people had in mind small *strategic* warheads when the miniaturization began, but once the technology was readily available, no one had any reason to make them big anymore. As a result, by the mid 1970s, no strategic warhead weighing more than 1,000 pounds was being planned, designed, or built.

Advances in other technologies made it possible to miniaturize most other components of strategic weapons as well, so that by the 1980s only perverse planning would produce a big weapon. The trend in technology dictated that one would build small weapons—and, just as important, so would one's opponents.

Defining Technology and Defining Arms Control

The unpredictable technological web that blurs the difference between a "strategic weapon" and a "tactical weapon" also makes it difficult to define a currency for arms control. In the SALT negotiations, strategic weapons were considered to be nuclear forces that the United States and the Soviet Union would use directly against each other's home territory—long-range inter- continental bombers, most submarine-launched ballistic missiles, and intercontinental ballistic missiles. Tactical nuclear weapons, such as short-range missiles and nuclear artillery, were consid- ered to be weapons used on the battlefield against tanks, troops, or ships at sea. (Tactical nuclear weapons have also been called "theater" or "intermediate-range" weapons.)

These definitions are important because they determine which weapons will be restricted by a treaty and which will not. The SALT treaties, for instance, limited only strategic arms (the "SA" in "SALT"), and as one might expect, the definition of "strate- gic" had to be negotiated. The Soviets and Americans dickered over, for example, whether U.S. fighter-bombers based in Europe or Soviet intermediate-range missiles should be counted. (Neither was.)

Including more types of weapons in SALT, of course, would have produced a more comprehensive agreement. It also would have been much more difficult to negotiate. The Soviets are re- luctant to count their intermediate-range forces in any treaty with the United States and NATO, because many of these mis- siles and bombers are planned for use against China. The United States has been just as reluctant to include its own European- based intermediate-range weapons, because they are supposed to deter a conventional attack by the Warsaw Pact nations.

But improvements in nuclear weapons technology are blurring the differences in size, capability, and most other characteristics that have enabled arms control negotiators to distinguish be- tween tactical and strategic weapons. Because nuclear weapons (and their delivery systems) are so much more efficient, many tactical weapons now have the range of strategic weapons, and many strategic weapons are becoming as compact and as mobile as tactical weapons.

So the two superpowers now face a choice: They can keep the old definitions, in which case arms control will not constrain many of the weapons that the United States and the Soviet Union could use against each other's homelands. Or the two countries can try to tackle the difficult task of controlling all nuclear weapons under a comprehensive treaty. Either way, there is bound to be trouble.

In the most recent talks, the United States and the Soviet Union have been spinning in circles around the problem of deciding which weapons should be included in a treaty. When the Carter Administration left office, the strategic and intermediate-range arms talks were separated. The Soviet Union and the United States had explicitly excluded intermediate nuclear forces from SALT II and from future strategic arms negotiations; they were to be limited by a separate agreement to be negotiated later, in what became known as the "INF talks" (for "intermediate-range nuclear forces"). The Soviets were then in the process of deploying a new intermediate-range missile, the SS-20. The NATO allies were threatening to deploy similar weapons by 1982 if the Soviets did not remove the new missiles. After the 1980 elections, the problem was left to the Reagan Administration, The United States followed through on its promise to deploy Pershing II missiles and cruise missiles in Europe. The Soviets responded by walking out of both the INF talks and the strategic arms negotiations.

After the 1982 elections, the Soviets came back to the negotiating table. Rather than try to settle the question of which weapons were strategic and which were tactical, the two countries agreed to fold them all into the same bundle. By this time space weapons such as the ASAT were attracting attention, so they were added to the negotiations, too.

The negotiators discovered, though, that reaching a single comprehensive agreement was no easier than reaching two or three separate agreements. This time the issue was the Soviets' insistence that the United States forswear all space-based defensive weapons, in exchange for a 50 percent reduction in Soviet offensive weapons. The United States refused, and the talks stalled again. No agreement could be reached, even under the pressure of the Reagan-Gorbachev summit at Geneva in November 1985.

Stuck on the space-based weapon controversy, the two leaders left Geneva, instructing their negotiators to try to reach an agreement on strategic and intermediate-range forces. But the new talks were not much more productive than the earlier talks.

Negotiators of both countries had accepted "in principle" the notion of a 50 percent cut in strategic weapons; however, as George Shultz said, "Don't ask me to agree in principle; it simply means we haven't agreed." The negotiations again ran into the problem of determining what constitutes a strategic weapon. The Soviets wanted to count any weapon that could reach the Soviet Union—including aircraft based on U.S. carriers and many U.S. fighters deployed with NATO—as a strategic weapon. American leaders objected, pointing out that under this definition the United States would be required to discard many weapons that the Soviet Union would be able to keep (for example, while the U.S. would give up its Pershing II intermediate-range missile, the Soviets would be able to keep SS-20s that it deployed against China). Also, the United States continued to hold out on the issue of space weapons.

At the Iceland Summit in November 1986, the currency problem emerged again. The U.S. and Soviet negotiators solved the intermediate-range missile problem by allowing the United States to keep 100 Pershing IIs in North America to match the 100 SS-20s the Soviets deployed in Siberia against China. But solving this problem only raised another: the Soviets have more *short*-range nuclear missiles than NATO (e.g., the U.S. Lance and the Soviet SS-21, SS-22, and SS-23, missiles with ranges of about 100 to 600 miles). Before the details of comparing these weapons could even be addressed, the talks collapsed when Reagan and Gorbachev began talking about a total ban on ballistic missiles.

Gorbachev put the talks back on track in February 1987, when he proposed that the United States and the Soviet Union agree simply to limit intermediate-range missiles, separately from strategic forces and space weapons. The Reagan Administration, eager to find something that would help put the Iran-Contra arms affair behind it, accepted the offer in principle, and the talks began again. The short-range missiles and questions concerning verification continued to complicate the negotiations.

But now there was an additional problem. By the time Gorbachev made his proposal, both the Soviets and the Americans had abandoned the SALT II limits on strategic weapons. The United States had concluded that the Soviets had already exceeded the limits of the treaty. (The SS-25 was just one Soviet violation; U.S. officials believed there were several others.) The United States had itself exceeded the SALT II limits in November 1986 by modifying its 131st B-52 bomber to carry cruise missiles; this put the United States over the SALT II limits on MIRVed weapons. And, the previous July, American representatives had told their Soviet counterparts that they would no longer discuss issues concerning the SALT II limits at the SCC in Geneva.

Thus, by any standard, SALT II was dead. This meant that any intermediate-range missile that was dismantled could be replaced by a strategic weapon, and, of course, any target an intermediate-range missile can hit, a strategic-missile can hit, too.

The logical response for the Soviets would be to replace any SS-20s they dismantled for the INF accord with SS-25s; the two missiles are quite similar. The Americans seemed to have overlooked this when they took up Gorbachev's overture. The Americans were preoccupied with the short-range missile problem; possibly the notion of replacing SS-20s with *longer-range* missiles was too obvious a countermeasure. Possibly the need for a foreign policy initiative in the aftermath of the Iran affair was too great an incentive. Or possibly U.S. officials felt that they could not reject a proposal that was originally their own. (The United States had proposed to ban intermediate weapons in earlier rounds at Geneva, when SALT II was still in effect.) *

To be fair, the problem is not just the fault of the negotiators. The definitions of "strategic" and "tactical" weapons are truly ambiguous. Add to this the question of British and French

---

* The intermediate-range missile treaty also contained other pitfalls.

After the United States definitively abandoned SALT II, the Soviet Union had a justification for abandoning the limits SALT imposed on adding additional warheads to existing missiles. One result was that the Soviets would be able to add four additional warheads to each of their SS-18s; this alone would compensate the Soviets for all of the warheads they would give up by scrapping their SS-20s. (The SS-18 was originally designed to carry fourteen warheads but was tested with only ten in order to comply with SALT.)

The Soviets could probably also add additional warheads to the SS-25. The SS-25 appears to be related to the SS-20, and since the SS-20 carries three warheads, it would seem that the SS-25 could be easily modified to carry three warheads as well.

forces (which are, incidentally, growing at an ever-faster rate as the two countries deploy MIRV-ed weapons), and the problem seems positively insoluble.

Recall the case of the Backfire bomber in the SALT talks. Not only did the Soviets and the United States differ about its range; the U.S. intelligence community itself was split on this issue. Air Force intelligence analysts insisted that the Backfire could attack the United States and then land at bases in Cuba. But Central Intelligence Agency analysts argued that even if this was technically feasible, the margin of safety would be so slim that the Russians would lack confidence in its practicality and would not plan such missions. (The CIA analysts also pointed out that the Backfire was deployed entirely in units assigned tactical missions, such as Soviet Naval Aviation and units attached to Soviet ground forces.) To complicate matters further, the intelligence community could not agree as to whether the Russians could refuel the Backfire in flight. (This would solve the range problem.)

Yet there were good reasons for the Air Force and the CIA to differ on the use and capabilities of the Backfire. No one in the intelligence community had a copy of the Backfire operator's manual, listing its true range. Rather, the analysts had information, most of it sketchy and of at least partially doubtful reliability, about such items as the weight of the aircraft, its fuel capacity, the efficiency of its engines, and so forth.

Figuring out how far a Backfire could fly was thus like figuring out how many miles per gallon one would get from a car one was considering buying. One can read the official Environmental Protection Agency estimate on the window, of course, but hardly anyone believes these figures. Instead, most car buyers probably ask whether the car has four or six cylinders, and whether it has fuel injection or a carburetor. They probably also consider the size of the car, and then crank in their own driving habits, bearing in mind that they will probably drive the car differently if it is a Porsche rather than a Buick.

Similarly, to estimate the range of a Backfire or any other Soviet aircraft, analysts use data on the characteristics of the bomber that have been acquired through various intelligence sources. Two analysts could disagree with each other at any step about the quality of the data (and whether some of it should be discarded), about what kind of model to use (one might depend mainly on weight estimates, another on engine characteristics), and about "softer" issues such as where the Soviets would base the Backfires in a crisis, and even how close a Soviet pilot would allow the fuel gauge to bump against "empty" before bailing out. Given this range of uncertainty, it is little wonder that even scrupulously professional analysts could disagree.

To save the SALT II treaty, Leonid Brezhnev gave the Americans his personal assurances that the Soviet Union would produce no more than thirty Backfires per year. This ceiling was supposed to have given the Soviets enough Backfires for tactical missions, and no more. Yet Soviet weapons were not the only ones blurring the distinction between strategic and tactical systems. At about the same time, the cruise missiles that the United States was deploying were also causing problems for arms control. The strategic and tactical versions of the same cruise missile are virtually identical and thus difficult to categorize under any arms control agreement.

The U.S. Navy, for example, deploys a tactical cruise missile called the "Tomahawk." In its tactical version, it carries a conventional warhead and thus would not be included within the SALT ceilings. Yet the Tomahawk can also carry a nuclear warhead, in which case the U.S. military itself would consider it a strategic weapon, and include it in its overall strategic war plans. There is almost no way to distinguish a tactical, nonnuclear Tomahawk from a strategic, nuclear Tomahawk. Of course, the Soviet version of the Tomahawk, which NATO calls the SS-N-21, presents the same problems.

The SS-20 gave some hint of the coming problems of defining a "strategic weapon." The Soviets began to deploy it in 1977; as we have already seen, it was the center of the breakdown in arms control negotiations in 1982. The SS-20 seems to have been intended to replace the obsolete SS-4 and SS-5 intermediate-range ballistic missiles (IRBMs) that the Soviets deployed in the early 1960s. The old missiles were almost certainly worn out, and the SS-20 gave the Soviet Union a chance to replace them and upgrade its intermediate-range forces at the same time.

The problem for the SALT II negotiators was that the SS-20 had a long range for an IRBM—5,000 kilometers, compared with the 4,000 kilometers for the SS-5 and 2,000 kilometers for the SS-4. The SS-20 carries three warheads, and some analysts thought that the Soviets could give it an intercontinental range by removing two of the warheads to lighten its load.

Even more troubling was the fact that the SS-20 was closely related to the SS-16, a three-stage ICBM that the Soviets tested between 1972 and 1976 but never deployed. The SS-20 was basically an SS-16 with the first stage left off. Or to put it another way, the SS-16 was an SS-20 with an additional stage tacked on. American analysts feared that the Soviets could deploy a large number of SS-20s, stockpile the third stage, and then convert them into ICBMs. The SALT II negotiators eventually settled the issue when the Soviets agreed not to test or deploy the SS-16. (The Soviets were not giving up much; the SS-16 does not seem to have worked well.) Yet to this day, hawkish analysts insist that the Soviets have stockpiled SS-16 conversion kits for their SS-20 force, and the Reagan Administration has accused the Soviets of violating the ban on testing and deploying the SS-16.

But this is just a preview of what is to come. All future arms limitation negotiations must face the fact that missile technology and missile performance have improved to the point where almost any modern IRBM will have the potential to be easily upgraded to an intercontinental missile. We know this because some American missiles, such as the Pershing II (ironically, the other half of the SS-20 controversy that led to the breakdown of the START talks), have the same potential. Indeed, some analysts have proposed that, rather than having the Air Force design a new small ICBM from scratch, the United States should have the Army convert its Pershing II into an ICBM. The main modification that would be necessary would be the addition of a third stage (shades of the SS-20).

Moreover, the convertibility of systems is not a problem limited to offensive weapons. In 1984 the Department of Defense announced that the Soviets had been testing a new antiaircraft missile, the SA-12, against ballistic missiles. The main differences between an antiaircraft and an antimissile missile system are the range of the interceptor and the sophistication of the tracking radar. (Missile warheads travel faster than aircraft and are likely to arrive in greater numbers, so the computer in the tracking radar must process a greater amount of information more quickly.)

Today, however, the differences between antimissile and anti-aircraft systems are disappearing as the cost of computing power falls. Electronic microprocessors are so cheap today that banks are giving away calculators to customers simply for opening a new checking account. The same technology makes it easier to build a missile defense radar today or to upgrade an antiaircraft defense system into an antimissile system.

The SALT I accords restrict the development of antimissile systems. For example, the radars used to control such systems can be built only along the periphery of the country, and each country can deploy only 100 interceptor missiles. Yet what will we do as antiaircraft missiles become faster and longer-ranged? What will we do as the radar systems supporting antiaircraft become powerful enough and sophisticated enough to track missile warheads?

To go one step farther into the future, consider high-energy lasers used for missile defense. Opponents of "Star Wars" want to ban such weapons. But the U.S. Navy is developing laser weapons to protect ships from swarms of aircraft and cruise missiles. The Defense Department claims that the Soviets are developing similar systems.

A tactical defense system against cruise missiles would, of course, require a much less powerful laser than a strategic anti-missile system. Even so, it would seem possible that eventually the naval laser system would have some potential to be used against missiles, too. It would simply be a matter of improving the efficiency of the laser, the output of the power source, or both. (There is precedent. Some of the newest antiaircraft missiles, such as the British Sea Wolf, can intercept missiles, too; in one test, in fact, the Sea Wolf successfully intercepted an artillery shell.) At that point, the question of whether the laser was a tactical or strategic system would depend merely on whether the laser was pointed horizontally or vertically. Yet no one has ever suggested that tactical lasers intended for defending an aircraft carrier should be restricted.[8]

To be sure, the distinction between "strategic" and "tactical" weapons was always somewhat artificial. Is a nuclear torpedo launched into the port of Philadelphia to destroy ships in the naval yard a strategic weapon or a tactical weapon? Many analysts believe such a strike was part of Soviet war planning during the late 1950s and early 1960s. What if the nuclear torpedo destroyed a good portion of Philadelphia, too? Would this be a strategic attack?

The problem of the vanishing distinction between tactical and strategic weapons is inherent in the technology. As missiles become more powerful and nuclear warheads smaller, tactical weapons will differ little from strategic weapons. The same is true of ballistic missiles, antimissile missiles, and directed-energy weapons. The result is trouble for arms control, if it depends on such distinctions.

Technology and the Sources of Controversy

Failing to appreciate the constraints technology poses on arms control can be dangerous. Keeping the lid on one form or another of weapons technology does not stop the development of similar technologies for other applications. Eventually, a civilian technology will become so commonplace that its conversion into military use will become simpler and simpler. At that point, arms control is at best extremely fragile and at worst a total sham.

Suppose that the Washington Conference *had* tried to control strategic bombers. As civilian airliners became more and more highly developed, the conversion of these airplanes into military attack aircraft would have become easier, and the ability of a country to "break out" of a strategic bomber ban would have grown. This prospect would have been even more troubling if bomber defenses had been neglected because bombers were nominally controlled by an international treaty.

Similarly, we could ban the testing of ASAT, but that is not going to stop the development of space shuttles by the United States and the Soviet Union. If we wait long enough, the conversion of a space shuttle into a highly effective military vehicle will become relatively simple. When this happens, the threat of a strategic breakout will be real indeed.

Not only is it easy to turn plowshares into swords; sometimes it is unnecessary because the plowshare itself is an effective weapon. Unless we could stop technology completely—which we cannot—we will have to learn to cope with a situation in which weapons, like everything else that is a product of technology, become ever more efficient.

CHAPTER SEVEN

Why People Believe in Arms Control:
The Elegant Argument

ONE way to justify arms control is to say that it will make arms races go away—simple problem, simple solution. This argument is usually sufficient for debates in the mass media arena of democratic politics, where a more complex argument is usually not possible.

Yet the debate over arms control, like most political debates over important issues, really takes place at two levels. Two-level debates often occur in politics. For example, the Democratic party sold the New Deal economic reforms by appealing to the popular ideals of equality, opportunity, and fairness, and by promising to reverse the Great Depression. Behind this rhetoric, though, were more than three decades of scholarly thought, mainly associated with the British economist John Maynard Keynes; of course, no one tried to teach the American voters Keynesian economics in order to get them to choose Roosevelt.*

The intellectual argument is not just for show; it is essential for the success of a policy. At some point the mass media demand some evidence that the policy will work. Also, the public expects policy proposals to have the support of at least some of the accepted experts in the field.

Arms control is usually sold by appealing to people's gut fear

* Indeed, as Keynes himself wrote, "Practical men, who believe themselves to be quite exempt from any intellectual influence, are usually the slaves of some defunct economist."

of war, but it is supported by a more complex argument that claims negotiated agreements limiting the deployment of weapons are an "elegant" solution—a clean, neat fix—to the complicated problem of arms races. The irony of this elegant argument for arms control is that its origins can be traced back to one of the most important individuals in the development of modern strategic nuclear weapons.

Games and Bombs

Almost everyone knows that Albert Einstein conceived the theory of relativity, which, as most people know at least intuitively, had something to do with the invention of the atomic bomb. But most people probably do not know who John von Neumann was—despite his role in developing not only nuclear weapons, but also the modern computer.

Von Neumann and Einstein were arguably the two most intelligent men of this century. Both were Jewish refugees who fled Europe before World War II, and both taught at Princeton University. Yet, in most respects, they were diametric opposites. Einstein was reticent, modest, and, in his later years especially, a pacifist. Von Neumann was flamboyant and cocky and was a frequent consultant to the armed services. Einstein had essentially completed his contribution to science by the time he was thirty-five years old; he spent the rest of his life trying unsuccessfully to formulate a general unified theory of physics. Von Neumann was a productive scholar up to his early death in 1957 at the age of fifty-three. Einstein's work was almost entirely theoretical; indeed, it was many years before some of his theories could be tested. Von Neumann, on the other hand, not only was a theoretical mathematician but was also intensely interested in practical matters.

One of these practical matters was computers. Von Neumann became involved with computers largely by chance, when he happened to run into Herman Goldstine at a train station in Aberdeen, Maryland, in the summer of 1944.

Goldstine worked at the University of Pennsylvania, building ENIAC, one of the first electronic computers; his research was supported by the Army, which needed to calculate firing tables for its artillery pieces. (A firing table tells a gunner the correct settings to aim for a given combination of ammunition, distance, and weather conditions; this setting is derived from a complex calculation of ballistics.) The problem was that, because of the war, the Army was developing new artillery systems faster than it could formulate firing tables for them. Changing the design of a gun changes its firing characteristics, so every time a new artillery system is developed, a new firing table is needed. The Army had already begun to use large mechanical calculators to develop firing tables, and Goldstine's contribution had been to improve the speed and accuracy of these calculators by replacing the mechanical apparatus with electrical switches.

Goldstine recognized von Neumann on the railway platform and struck up a conversation; soon the two men were talking shop, which led Goldstine to describe his work on the new electronic computer. Von Neumann quickly appreciated the significance of Goldstine's work. Von Neumann was engaged in a program that required elaborate calculations—the Manhattan Project. In those days, most of these calculations were done by hand by graduate students working in teams of two, one checking the other. This could require weeks of dog work, and any machine that could reduce this drudgery was a good thing.[1]

Following his chance encounter with Goldstine, von Neumann started visiting the computer lab at the University of Pennsylvania frequently, and soon became one of the leading figures in computer development. Within a few years, he changed the way people thought about computers, showing that computers were not merely highly capable calculators, but could also be the basis for a unique science—artificial intelligence, machine logic, and so on. But von Neumann's most important contribution was probably the computer "program."

The first computers were simply mechanical devices that, through a system of cogs and gears, multiplied or added figures. The "logic" of the machine was fixed in the layout of the cogs and gears; to calculate $1 + 1$, for example, a gear somewhere in the machine might turn twice, registering "2" on a ratcheting mechanism. Electronic computers, such as ENIAC, used electrical switches in the form of vacuum tubes. This made calculating faster, but even these computers had their logic built into the hardware (i.e., the electrical connections of the machine); once set up, the machine could operate only according to one set of commands. To change the logic, the operator had to change the settings of the switches, often a lengthy process.

Von Neumann's insight was to treat the logic of a math problem like data. Computers were already fed data in the form of the numbers plugged into a statistical or mathematical calculation. The usual method was to code them on punch cards or paper tape, and then allow the machine to "read" them. (Today we code such data on magnetic tape or magnetic disks, but the principle is still the same.) Why not, thought von Neumann, build a machine that had a large number of switches set to random positions, and then feed in a set of logic statements? The machine would set its own switches according to these instructions, read in the data, and solve the problem according to the instructions that it had been fed.

Every computer built since—including the one with which this book is being written—has used von Neumann's invention. We take computer programs for granted today, but to appreciate the importance of the idea, imagine rewiring a personal computer each time one wanted to switch from, say, balancing a spreadsheet on *Lotus 1-2-3* to flying loops on *Flight Simulator*.

Von Neumann's work on computers came too late to help the Manhattan Project. Most of the calculations had already been done. However, he understood how the computer would have speeded the design of the atomic bomb; and as a result, one of the first tasks of the programmable computer was to design the hydrogen bomb.

Designing a hydrogen bomb is much more complicated than the simple description given earlier might lead one to believe. Assume that one has the uranium or plutonium, the explosives, and the lithium deuteride necessary for a nuclear weapon. How much fissile material is enough? How much energy must the fission trigger produce? How far away from the fission bomb trigger should the fusion fuel be located? The answers require precise calculations; guess wrong, and a neutron or gamma ray might arrive at its destination a few nanoseconds before it is supposed to, and the immutable laws of physics dictate that the result will be a fizzle.*

The scientists building the first thermonuclear weapons were exploring unknown territory. Even after the Greenhouse tests provided some of the basic data of fusion reactions, the scientists still had to determine the detailed specifications for a working Teller-Ulam device. There were two main problems: designing a fission trigger that would produce enough of the right types of energy for fusion, and determining how to arrange the trigger and the fusion fuels so that the hydrogen isotopes would be compressed and ignited before the whole assembly was destroyed by the explosion of the fission trigger. A number of combinations of triggers, fusion fuels, and geometries in which the two are arranged are possible, and working through the mathematics for each combination is a problem of solving a complicated system of simultaneous equations. It was here that von Neumann's computer was invaluable. The first hydrogen bomb simply could not have been built when it was were it not for the programmable computer.

Since then, computer development has been closely linked to strategic weapons. Many of the difficulties of strategic warfare—guidance systems, warhead designs, reconnaissance—are primarily problems in processing large amounts of information quickly, and this is precisely where computers excel.

It is the computer, combined with inertial guidance, that makes possible the incredible accuracy of modern strategic weapons, which in turn makes it theoretically possible for one nuclear power to launch a disarming strike against its opponent. It is this

* Even professional bomb builders can err, as the bomb builders at Lawrence Livermore Laboratory (the second nuclear weapons lab established in the United States) discovered when they tested their first hydrogen bomb. In the lab's early years, the scientists were mainly younger individuals who had participated in the first nuclear weapons tests but had not designed a nuclear weapon. They understood the basics of bomb building well, but were less familiar with the fine points. These Young Turks were determined to be daring, designing bombs that were smaller and more efficient than those being built by their competitors at Los Alamos. Unfortunately, they were too daring; in trying to shave the mass of their bombs to a minimum, they went too far. In their first tests the Livermore bombs had barely enough yield to blow off the tops of the towers on which they were mounted.

threat of such "surgical strikes" that makes nuclear war more plausible. On the other hand, it is the computer, combined with microwave technology, that makes early-warning radars feasible, which in turn make such disarming strikes implausible. Without the computer, strategic weapons and nuclear war would not exist, and it was largely John von Neumann who made computers what they are today.

Yet von Neumann was responsible not only for the development of nuclear weapons; he is also largely responsible for how we *think* about nuclear weapons. A von Neumann invention, "game theory," underlies many of our concepts of both deterrence and arms control.

Von Neumann's explanation of human action is what one might expect from a mathematician with worldly interests. Game theory is usually written in symbols and equations; it has the "topography" of physics and, like physics, is constructed deductively: One begins with explicit assumptions about how people behave, works through a series of logical steps, and arrives at a conclusion about what they will do in particular situations.

Game theory's origins lie in gambling. As most gamblers (or, at least, most successful gamblers) know, in any game of chance there is a strategy that will give the player the best possible odds and, hence, the biggest payoff. Von Neumann was quick to see that gambling theory, which describes this strategy when a player is competing against some unchanging opponent ("the house," "nature," or just "the odds") could be adapted to explain the best strategy in games in which a person is competing against another person (as in, say, poker). The main difference, said von Neumann, is that in games with two or more people, the best strategy often depends on what the opponent decides to do.

If, as von Neumann assumed, people usually act in their own best interest, such a theory—game theory—could be used to explain other competitive situations, such as labor-management negotiations or diplomatic bargaining. Indeed, said von Neumann, just as one can predict the behavior of successful gamblers, one should be able to predict the winner, the loser, and the outcome of a game or bargaining session. Von Neumann published his first papers on game theory in 1928. Not many people paid attention to the theory at first, and he laid the idea aside for a few years while he pursued quantum mechanics.[2]

Von Neumann turned back to game theory in the mid-1940s, when he collaborated with his economist friend, Oskar Morgenstern, to write *The Theory of Games and Economic Behavior*.[3] By this time, the audience for game theory was better, in large part because of the development of operations research.

Operations research started in World War II, when the Royal Air Force's Bomber Command began planning strikes against Germany. The main idea in strategic bombing is to destroy the enemy's industrial base, and operations research used economic statistics and data on damage from previous bombing missions to plan later missions for the greatest effect. When the United States entered the war, the U.S. Army Air Corps established a similar program. (The U.S. program was called operations "analysis," to avoid the stigma of appearing too academic.)[4]

Operations analysis seemed successful enough that, after the war, General H. H. "Hap" Arnold, the first Chief of Staff of the newly created U.S. Air Force, helped establish a nonprofit consulting company that would continue the program in peacetime. This company eventually became the Rand Corporation (for Research *and* Development), the first of the private "think tanks."[5]

In time, Rand moved from analyzing bombing tactics to analyzing bombing strategy, and from there it was a short step to analyzing bombing *policy*—deterrence, arms control, and the other facets of grand strategy in the nuclear age. It was here that the operations analysts turned to von Neumann's invention. Many of them, being mathematicians, statisticians, and economists, were already familiar with game theory. It fit their style (lots of symbols, abstractions, and deductive thinking), and it had the seal of approval of John von Neumann, who had considerable prestige in military circles.

Also, game theory allowed them to approach these issues systematically. Suppose, for example, that you are the President and want to deter the Soviet Union from attacking the United States. Should you buy Force A, with lots of bombers and a few airfields, or Force B, with a few bombers and lots of airfields?

Force A would be a powerful offensive force but would be relatively vulnerable; concentrating many bombers on a few airfields would give the Soviets a good target. In a crisis, the Soviets might be enticed to attack, thinking that they could destroy most or all of the American bombers. Force B, though weaker, might be a better deterrent because it would be invulnerable to most Soviet attacks; Soviet leaders would know that the United States would always have some capability to retaliate.

Rand actually developed such studies on bomber basing during the 1950s. At the time, the United States did have a large number of bombers operating from a relatively small number of bases. Strategic Air Command (SAC) officials cared little about protecting U.S. strategic forces; their attention was focused on offensive capabilities. But the author of the Rand studies, a mathematician named Albert Wohlstetter, made the case for reducing vulnerability, and subsequently the United States built more airfields, located its land-based missiles in silos, put more of its strategic missiles into submarines, and so forth.[6]

Game theory was not really as objective a system of analysis as its proponents claimed (it depended heavily on the assumptions an analyst used), but it did become a way for analysts to explain and justify their recommendations to policymakers. Even more important, it influenced many of the thinkers who were reshaping U.S. arms control policy in the early 1960s, such as the Cambridge group.

For example, consider the grand policy of the nuclear age: deterrence. As Bernard Brodie argued in *The Absolute Weapon*, since a foolproof defense against nuclear weapons seemed impossible, the only way to protect a country from atomic attack was the threat of retaliation. The operations analysts had a neat game-theory explanation of nuclear deterrence and the conditions necessary for it to work. It came to be called "Chicken," after the teenage motor sport reputed to be popular during the hot-rod era.

In Chicken, two adversaries are presented with a choice: either pressing ahead full-throttle or swerving off the road. The costs of swerving are considerable (chicken!), but the potential costs of not swerving (a trip to the hospital or possibly the mortuary) are even greater. Hence, said the game theorists, so long as the dangers were clear and both drivers followed the same rationale, both would swerve—which explained why hot-rodders are able to live to a ripe old age.

Chicken was supposed to show policymakers that deterrence could prevent nuclear war, but only if both sides had a credible threat to retaliate. Without such a threat, the game theorists said, an opponent might think it could get away with a nuclear strike. This was why the arms control thinkers of the early 1960s (many of whom had backgrounds in economics and knew about game theory) decided to concentrate on using arms control as a means to reduce the likelihood of either the United States or the Soviet Union executing a disarming first strike, which would negate the opponent's ability to retaliate. Arms control was sup-posed to ensure that both countries would remain chicken.

It is significant that game theorists would often render the United States and the Soviet Union as abstractions—Country A and Country B, for example. In part, this reflected their scien-tific or academic backgrounds. But it also reflected the beliefs that many of them held on international politics. They believed that international relationships could and should be managed, and not merely left to random chance. Arms control was sup-posed to be a method for coordinating the policies of the United States and the Soviet Union so that the stalemate of deterrence held.

Yet the game theorists also had another rationale for arms control, which arose from their explanation of why arms races occur in the first place. This came to be called the "Prisoner's Dilemma," after the following story:

Two suspects are arrested for a burglary and locked in sep-arate interrogation rooms. They cannot communicate with each other in any way. The district attorney tells each of them that if he implicates his partner, the state will give him a reduced sen-tence—say, a heavy fine and probation. However, if he is unco-operative and his partner confesses first, the prisoner will bear the full brunt of the law—say, ten years.

Despite the DA's pitch, the prisoner knows his best hope is if both he and his partner keep quiet; then the state may be un-able to convict either of them, and they may both go free. Unfortunately for the prisoners, neither can trust the other to keep mum—they cannot confer with each other, and probably no one is as suspicious of a thief as another thief. Since neither prisoner can take the chance of being burned by his partner and getting stuck with a ten-year sentence, the most likely outcome is that they will *both* confess to the crime.

This is called the "Prisoner's Dilemma" because the logical outcome of the situation is perverse—from the viewpoint of a game theorist, a civil libertarian, and, of course, the prisoners. It is perverse because neither prisoner is making out as well as he could. If they both kept quiet, both could go free. The problem is that the two prisoners cannot talk to each other. If they could, they would quickly arrive at the bargain that would make them both better off. (And this, of course, is precisely why the DA wants to keep the two suspects isolated from each other.)[7]

The game theorists saw an analogy between the Prisoner's Dilemma and the plight of two countries in an arms race. For the countries, the choice is between building and not building more arms. Like the two prisoners who would both be better off not confessing, the two countries would probably be better off if neither side built more arms; an arms race would only cost considerable amounts of money and would not change the military balance appreciably. For example, according to the game theorists, in 1949, after the United States and the Soviet Union had both developed the atomic bomb, neither could trust the other to refrain from developing thermonuclear weapons. So both went on to develop the hydrogen bomb, even though it made neither country better off than before; the main result was that billions of dollars were spent. If only the Soviet Union and the United States would simply negotiate with each other in good faith, the game theorists said, the two countries would quickly agree that arms control would leave them both better off.

This argument is compelling because it is "elegant." All of the pieces of the arms control bargain seem to slip into place so easily. According to the theory, it is not necessary to *persuade* leaders not to build weapons; assuming that they truly want security and want it at the lowest possible price, simply agreeing to negotiate should lead to a solution. Not only will arms control make this outcome possible; it is only the *lack* of arms control negotiations that creates the unnatural condition of an arms race.

Von Neumann's brainchild, game theory, has had more than its share of critics. Most of them object to its characterization of man as purely economic man, who always acts in his rational self-interest. Yet the idea of the arms race as an unnatural paradox that could be avoided has become ingrained in our politics. Even the most conservative politicians these days seem to agree that arms control, with tough-minded negotiators on the American side, could slow the arms race. Witness Ronald Reagan, who came into office arguing that the United States should negotiate not just a ceiling on strategic weapons, but reductions.

The problem with a good theory is that facts sometimes get in the way. In the case of the Prisoner's Dilemma, the problem is not the logic of the elegant argument for arms control, but simply the fact that countries usually have not gone into negotiations with the motivations that the argument assumes they have. The archives and the private correspondence of arms control negotiators suggest that countries do not enter negotiations because they want to avoid an arms race. Rather, the leader of at least one country usually believes another country is about to start an arms buildup that his own nation cannot match.

As a result, arms control negotiations do not produce a "natural solution" in which the deployment of additional weapons is averted. Instead, leaders of the threatened country usually determine the maximum degree to which they can meet the perceived threat, and then try to get their opponent to bargain away as much of its advantage as possible. The net effect is that the negotiations generally establish—and sometimes raise—the *minimum* number of weapons a country will deploy.

Consider the naval treaties. Of the three great naval powers in 1921, only Japan was truly committed to an arms race. The United States, despite the official commitment to its 1916 naval program and a big fleet, probably would not have followed through with its plans. Britain was even more reluctant. Both governments had incentives to limit naval construction: the postwar economic slump and the demands from war-weary electorates for butter rather than guns, to name just two. As one might expect, the United States and Britain pressed for naval arms control, while Japan was reluctant.

Most accounts of the Washington Treaty overlook these motives and paint the situation as one in which an arms race was imminent. The reason for the confusion is that, though the United States and Great Britain had policies for building big navies, it is one thing to authorize the construction of a ship and quite another to appropriate the money necessary to actually build it.

For example, in the United States, congressional approval of a weapon is a two-part process: first each house must authorize the program; then the money necessary to carry out the policies must be appropriated. Sometimes the two procedures can get blurred; authorization legislation is often debated in the universally understood language of money, and appropriations are often debated in terms of how wisely the money will be spent. Be that as it may, this two-part procedure is followed in most modern political systems.*

The naval program the U.S. Congress passed in 1916 was an authorization bill. But Congress delayed and stretched out the necessary appropriations. Much of the money that the United States was to have spent on battleships and cruisers during World War I had been diverted to destroyers, which the Allies had desperately needed to protect convoys from German U-boats. The Navy had never caught up with its original production schedule, and once the war was over, appropriations for naval construction were harder to come by. By 1921 the program was languishing.[8]

Even supporters of a strong navy were skeptical that they would ever obtain the necessary funding. For example, Charles Evans Hughes wrote in his memoirs:

> I kept in touch with Congress as closely as possible. The response to the drive of public opinion had demonstrated that there was no possibility that Congress would make the appropriations necessary to

---

* Most likely the split between authorizations and appropriations occurs even in dictatorial systems, such as the Soviet Union. In the Soviet system, weapons systems are proposed and developed by the Ministry of Defense but shaped by the economic program of the State Planning Commission (Gosplan), with each agency having its representatives in the Communist party to give it political clout. This pattern probably occurs wherever government budgets are big enough that official spending itself becomes a political issue.

carry out even the existing building program, to say nothing of the additional building programs which the competition among the leading naval powers would require. President Harding was convinced of this. Senator [Henry Cabot, Sr.] Lodge, who had the reputation of being the "big navy" leader in the Senate, came to that conclusion, and Senator [Oscar] Underwood . . . the minority leader, had the same view.[9]

The situation was much the same in Great Britain. British leaders knew their country would not compete in a naval arms race. Immediately after the war, the British halted all naval programs, including the construction of three sister ships to the *Hood*, which were partially completed in the docks. The Cabinet completely rejected the Navy's requests for new capital ship construction in 1919 and 1920. It agreed in 1921 to fund four new battle cruisers, but only after making clear that no more would be built for the foreseeable future.[10]

Thus, the British accepted the invitation to Washington, unwilling to match the other major sea powers in construction. According to the official records (released many years later), the British went to Washington because they hoped that arms control would reduce the threat from foreign navies, which they were not willing to match.

Unfortunately, though the British and the Americans were eager to freeze battleship construction, the Japanese were not. Recall that Japan had already invested large sums of money in nearly completed ships. The British and the Americans wanted a complete and immediate freeze, but the Japanese would not go along; the *Mutsu* controversy was one manifestation of their reluctance. The United States and Great Britain decided that half a loaf was better than none, and so they agreed to allow the Japanese to keep the *Mutsu*, even though this would require them to build additional new ships if they were to keep the original displacement ratios. A member of the British Cabinet cabled the delegation in Washington:

> Committee of Imperial Defense further considered subject of your telegram No. 73 this morning. First we have signified our agreement to the original American proposal of battleship strength, and that is still our definite policy. But rather than lose the battleship agreement altogether through Japanese reluctance we should

be willing to defer to American and Japanese wishes [the U.S. delegation had already conceded the point] for the construction of the "Mutsu," two additional "Marylands," and two of the new "Hoods" which are already in hand and start the ten years' holiday on a somewhat higher basis. You will realize that this involves us in serious expenditure which we had hoped to avoid.[11]

Though the treaty was finally adopted, throughout the 1920s and most of the 1930s, neither Britain nor the United States deployed a "treaty navy," one as large as each was permitted under the 5:5:3 agreement. In other words, the ceilings imposed by the Washington Treaty really were irrelevant for the British and Americans, because support for a major naval buildup just did not exist in either country.

As one might expect, not only was Japan the country least willing to accept a freeze on major ships; it was also the worst violator of the naval agreements. In some cases, as in limitations on the sizes of cruisers, Japan seems to have ignored the limitations completely. And, in the end, it was Japan that finally withdrew from the arms control agreements completely in 1937.[12]

One irony of the Washington Conference is that British and American leaders both seem to have known they would be unable to carry out their announced naval programs, but each feared that the other would. The Washington accords had little real effect on Britain and the United States; the treaty merely confirmed political reality within each country. But the Japanese, whose intention to build was real, were not effectively restrained. Thus, the Washington Treaty, perhaps the most celebrated arms control agreement of all, may have been, in reality, irrelevant.

The same pattern appeared in the SALT negotiations fifty years later. In this case, we do not know what the Soviet leaders were saying to each other, but we do know what the Americans were thinking. Henry Kissinger saw SALT as part of détente, and arms control as useful to the extent that it reduced the likelihood of a war between the Soviet Union and the United States. He did not, however, see arms control as a way to prevent the United States from stumbling into an arms race that it would be better off to avoid. If anything, American leaders in 1969 believed the Soviet Union had a potential advantage in the strategic arms race, and any measure that could slow the Soviet buildup would be welcome.

Arms control supporters—especially those who believe in the elegant argument—like to say that SALT I averted a Soviet-American ABM arms race. They often go so far as to say that the ABM Treaty, the part of SALT I limiting ballistic missile defenses, was the single most important arms control agreement of the 1970s. Yet, in truth, SALT I did not avert an ABM race at all; no race could have taken place, simply because the United States was unwilling to participate.

The U.S. Senate approved the construction of the first two ABM bases by the narrowest possible margin—the vote was a 49–49 tie, with the deadlock broken by Vice President Spiro Agnew. Henry Kissinger had argued that he needed the ABM as a card to play in his negotiations with the Soviets. Technically, Kissinger got his card. But it was worthless, because everyone could see that any American threat to build a significant ABM system was a sham. Soviets can read the newspapers as well as we can, and they probably knew that the support necessary to build a full ABM system just did not exist in the Congress.

In the end, the treaty allowed each country to build just two ABM bases. Later, Congress canceled one of the two planned U.S. bases; the treaty was modified so that each country was permitted to have just one base. The remaining American ABM base was retired just one year after it was activated—hardly the mark of a country committed to a race.

It is impossible to determine how many ABMs or ICBMs the Soviets planned to build in the absence of SALT. We do know, however, what top Soviet military officials write to each other in their professional journals. The most frequent justification they give for arms control is that they believe it might cap the American technological advantage—not that it will stabilize Soviet-American relations, or promote deterrence, or anything else.

So arms control in both the Washington Treaty and SALT I did little to avert an arms race. Rather, it simply allowed the countries that were determined to arm to go ahead and arm, and permitted the countries that were unwilling to arm to fool themselves into thinking that they had reduced the threat presented by their opponent.

The same pattern is playing true today. The Reagan Administration stalled on arms control for two years in order to concentrate on modernizing U.S. strategic forces. When it finally addressed arms control in mid-1982, two issues shaped the proposal the United States offered.

First, many administration officials wanted to eliminate the advantage SALT I had allowed the Soviet Union in big ICBMs. (This became known as the "throw-weight issue," referring to the greater military payload the Soviets were able to lift with their large ICBMs.) Once the Soviets mastered MIRV technology and improved their missile guidance systems, the large Soviet ICBMs permitted the Soviet Union to deploy enough fast, accurate warheads to put the U.S. Minuteman force at risk.

Second, the United States had revised its own policy for strategic deterrence. The Reagan Administration (in truth, continuing a line of thinking started during the Carter Administration) had concluded that the best way to deter the Soviets was not by threatening to destroy the Soviet economy and society, but by threatening to destroy Soviet military forces and the political leadership of the Soviet Union. This policy, which came to be called a "countervailing strategy," was designed to convince the Soviets that they could not achieve their objectives in a nuclear war and would be hurt in the areas they valued most (namely, preserving the rule of the Communist Party and maintaining Soviet military power).

Previously, U.S. war plans had targeted the Soviet economy—factories, generating plants, and the like. The new policy required the United States to be able to destroy Soviet strategic forces (e.g., ICBM silos) and the underground bunkers in which Soviet leaders would take shelter during a nuclear war. Thus, the United States had to restructure its strategic forces and deploy new types of weapons; the United States could make do with fewer weapons than before, but these weapons had to be more accurate. (There are fewer military and political targets in the Soviet Union than there are factories and generating plants, but they tend to be better protected.) The revised targeting plans, in turn, shaped the proposals U.S. representatives offered the Soviets in the START negotiations.[13]

The administration's proposals for strategic arms control were unveiled by President Reagan in a speech he gave at Eureka College in May 1982: a limit of 5,000 warheads on each side, a limit of 2,500 of these warheads to be permitted on land-based missiles, and a limit of 850 ballistic missiles total. At the time the proposal was offered, some critics of the Reagan Administration accused the President of playing a joker—offering a plan that played to the public's professed desire for cuts, but was known to be unacceptable to the Soviets. Yet, in truth, the Eureka proposal was entirely consistent with U.S. strategic policy. The new U.S. war plans could tolerate lower limits on warheads, so long as they allowed the U.S. to deploy the new higher-accuracy warheads (which the proposal did). Meanwhile, the plans would have also required the Soviets to limit their own force of SS-18 and SS-19 high-accuracy warheads.[14]

The administration's posturing may seem cynical, but in fact it only reflected political reality. Any plan that constrained the program necessary for the new strategic policy (and remember, this policy originated in the Carter Administration) would have cost the administration the support of the uniformed military services, civilian officials in the Defense Department, and anyone else who had a stake in the countervailing doctrine.

It seems that arms control is hardly an "elegant solution" for the prisoners of an arms race. There is no natural incentive for countries to cut back on their defense programs even if they have the opportunity to coordinate their policies with each other; rather, arms control negotiations seem to provide the lubricant that allows countries to slip easily into the policies they have already decided for themselves. Von Neumann and other game theorists were not *wrong;* it is just that there are other factors— military strategy, not to mention pork-barrel politics, bargaining in the domestic political arena, and so on—that put a floor underneath a country's military deployments, arms control or no arms control.

If this is so, does arms control have a place in U.S. policy at all? In fact, it might. Arms control might not reduce the expense of the arms race, the cost of weapons, or the size of the military forces countries deploy, but it can reduce the probability and costs of war. To see how, one must first reconsider the very definition of "arms control."

CHAPTER EIGHT

Arms Control That Works

So far, the case for arms control must appear bleak. Yet, arms control can play an important role in American foreign policy.

One reason I have concentrated so heavily on debunking the claims of arms control advocates is that the arguments of arms control opponents hardly need debunking at all. Most of them believe that the Soviets cannot be trusted; that they will cheat on any agreement; that arms control only weakens the United States in the face of Soviet aggressive tendencies; and so on. These arguments depend almost entirely on a characterization of the Soviet leadership as a mob of ogres.

But this is unprovable. A Soviet "mentality," "mindset," or "operational code" probably does not exist any more than an American version does. We know little of the inner workings of the Kremlin. We know little about the basic nature—if such a thing even exists—of the Soviet ruling elite. Was Georgi Romanov, one of the contenders for the post of General Secretary in the early 1980s, really more aggressive than Mikhail Gorbachev? Or was Gorbachev just more subtle and sophisticated (and, hence, more dangerous) than Romanov? And even if one could answer such questions as these, how would the answers translate into predictions of Soviet policy? Into prescriptions for American responses? To date, *no one* in the United States has a remarkable record for explaining the behavior of the Soviet Union, let alone predicting it.

154

Consider the forecasts produced by the U.S. intelligence community about Soviet strategic forces during the past thirty years. During that time, the intelligence community sometimes overestimated Soviet missile deployments (from 1957 to 1962), sometimes underestimated them (from 1964 to 1972), and sometimes was correct (in the early 1960s and late 1970s).[1] The reasons for the errors ranged from poor intelligence data to the difficulty of choosing an estimate when the intelligence community's top analysts, all with solid credentials and sound arguments, could not themselves reach a consensus. Whatever the case, it is simply facile to base a policy as important as arms control on something as unsubstantial as our interpretation of "Soviet intentions," which is what the anti-arms control arguments usually do.*

The arguments for arms control, on the other hand, have been much more sophisticated, and their proposed solutions to the arms race seem much more plausible. The "only" problem has been that arms control has failed to produce what has been promised. Arms control does not save money; it does not limit arms; it does not control weapon technology; and it often creates, rather than reduces, tension and ill will between countries.

In fact, arms control supporters have probably done at least as

---

* Indeed, one has to wonder whether anything that could be called "Soviet intentions" really exists, except perhaps in the broadest sense of the word. Soviet elites may share some vaguely defined common values: commitment to the security of the Soviet Union, hope for the development of the Soviet economy, a desire to keep the Party in control, and, most likely, a hope that the elites continue to enjoy the comforts and perquisites of their position. American leaders may share similar values for their country. It is difficult to say how this helps predict the behavior of the Soviet Union or the United States.

An intelligence analyst should pity his counterparts in the Soviet Union. Soviet analysts have access to enormous computer files of American voting behavior and public opinion. They have the benefit of "insider stories" that appear from time to time in the *Washington Post*. They have uncensored biographies of former American officials. Yet how would any analyst in the KGB or the Foreign Ministry in 1975 have predicted that a farmer from Georgia would be elected President in 1976; that such a moderately liberal President would, three years later, propose and initiate the largest rearmament program for the United States since the Vietnam War; and that he would lose office by a landslide in 1980 to a retired Hollywood actor? Imagine, then, the Soviets trying to base their arms control policy on "American intentions."

much damage to their cause as have their opponents, simply by being too ambitious in the kinds of controls they promote and the promises they make. Politics and technology limit the agreements that are feasible at any given moment; ignore this fact, and arms control will be oversold and discredited. Even worse, failing to understand the limits of arms control can prove positively harmful to American international interests.

So what kinds of arms control *do* work?

The real objective of arms control is not just to eliminate arms but to eliminate, or at least to minimize, the costs—the death and destruction of war—that weapons make possible. Though it would be desirable (and certainly cheaper) if a country did not have to deploy weapons at all, arms "control" in the literal sense (i.e., controlling them so that they are not used) may, in the end, be better, if only because its prospects for success are greater.

What follows are accounts of two international agreements that have met this standard. They are not the most widely known treaties, but they have probably produced more tangible progress in limiting conflict and reducing tension between the superpowers than all of the other treaties combined.

The Incidents at Sea Agreement

Beginning in the mid-1960s, an increasing number of American naval officers reported having been "harassed" by Soviet ships while on maneuvers. Sometimes a Soviet destroyer or cruiser would cut across the path of an American formation and refuse to yield the right of way, even if the international rules of navigation stipulated that it should. So the Americans would have to take evasive action, possibly breaking formation. Or sometimes a Soviet ship would train its guns or fire-control radars on the American ships, as though it were about to open fire. Or, to give the worst situation, sometimes a Soviet ship would get in the way of an American aircraft carrier as it was sending aloft or recovering its airplanes.

This game of "chicken of the sea" could be thought of as just another example of superpower sparring, harmless enough if it stopped at simple harassment. However, such stunts can be extremely dangerous. The threat of collision, of course, is obvious, but what most alarmed American captains was Soviet interference with our aircraft carriers during flight operations. If the carrier were forced to take evasive actions in order to avoid a Soviet ship while an aircraft was taking off or landing, more than just the pilot and crew of the aircraft would be in danger. During flight operations, the decks of carriers are filled with airplanes, not to mention ammunition and fuel. A crash landing in the midst of 1,000-pound bombs and aviation gas could endanger the entire ship.

To be sure, the Soviets had their own list of complaints about incidents in which American ships stunted with their Soviet counterparts. They cited numerous cases in which American naval aircraft buzzed their ships. ("Buzzing," a word that brings to mind annoying mosquitoes on a summer evening, does not quite do justice to the Soviet perspective. Imagine a jet aircraft, afterburners roaring so loudly that you feel the concussion over your entire body, passing twenty or thirty feet above the mast of your ship, and you have a better appreciation of the complaint.) The Soviets complained further about the American use of sonar buoys, floating devices that aircraft drop into the sea to track a submarine suspected to be in the area. The buoys emit loud "pinging" noises that, when reflected off a submarine, can be analyzed with listening devices to locate its position. Soviet submarine crews are said to find the "pinging" most obnoxious.

The number of incidents increased throughout the rest of the decade. By the end of the 1960s there were about 100 per year.[2] The United States was the first to react, firing a series of formal protests to the Soviet government. At first the Soviets simply denied such incidents even occurred; later they charged that the American ships were at fault. The worst of the incidents occurred in May 1967, when the American destroyer *Walker* met its Soviet counterpart *Bessledniy* in the Sea of Japan. The two ships actually scraped hulls, removing some paint in the process. By this time, U.S. officials were sufficiently concerned to propose that the two countries negotiate an agreement to avert such encounters. The Soviets ignored the overture.

Looking back, it can be understood how the dispute occurred. The Russians were only a minor sea power for most of this century. For decades, the Soviet Navy consisted of hand-me-down ships inherited from the czarist regime. Part of the reason for the Soviets' neglect of the Navy was that geography dictates that the Soviet Union be mainly a land power. Part was that Soviet leaders were always somewhat suspicious of the Navy as harboring counterrevolutionary tendencies. Stalin toyed with the idea of building a navy throughout the 1930s and 1940s—the Soviets even laid down the keels for a series of battleships—but nothing materialized until the early 1950s, when the Soviet Union began to build the Sverdlov-class cruisers. Alas, Stalin died, and the cruisers that were not already completed or almost fitted out were scrapped. The Soviets did not build another large warship until the "Kynda" class missile cruiser Grozny was launched in 1962.[3]

The Soviets really got serious about navy-building in the mid-1960s, starting a massive naval program that continues to this day. The growth of the Soviet Navy was reflected in the deployments of its ships on the high seas, away from their normal bases (in naval terms, "out of area"). In 1960, Soviet ships accounted for just 5,000 "ship days" out of area (one ship out of area for one day equals one "ship day"). By the early 1970s, this presence on the high seas had multiplied by almost a factor of ten.[4] So it was inevitable that American ships would meet their Soviet counterparts at some point.

Unfortunately, ships in newly emergent navies are usually commanded by newly emergent officers. The Soviet captains, feeling their oats, were eager to prove themselves as sailors. Yet the Soviet commanders were ill-prepared. Handling any large ship is a complex art that takes time to learn, let alone to teach to an entire corps of officers. (Some idea of the inexperience of the Soviet officers is given by the fact that, at least in the early 1970s, the Soviet Navy awarded them special pins for making "extended cruises"—typically defined as requiring two weeks from home port.)

The American offer to negotiate remained on the table until 1970, when the Soviet government delivered a diplomatic note proposing that negotiations be opened the following year. The United States accepted the offer, the delegations from the two countries assembled in Moscow in June 1971, and the negotiations proceeded quickly. The main disagreement was that the Soviets wanted to establish a specific distance that ships would have to maintain between each other, while the United States did not. In the end, the Soviets conceded the point. The basic agreement was settled in less than a year, and the formal treaty was signed during the Nixon-Brezhnev summit meeting of May 1972.[5]

Why was negotiating this treaty so easy? First, the treaty itself was extraordinarily simple. Its entire text fills just a few pages. It is, in fact, wholly derivative; aside from a passage prohibiting such annoyances as training guns or missile launchers on an opponent's ships, or illuminating an opponent's bridge with powerful searchlights, the agreement is mainly a reaffirmation of the long-established "Rules of the Road" for navigation on the high seas.[6]

Second, the treaty was an all-win, no-lose proposition for both countries. Both stood to have specific, concrete grievances addressed. The gains for the United States were readily apparent: the treaty kept the Soviet Navy away from U.S. aircraft carriers. It is more difficult to ascertain exactly why the Soviets were suddenly willing to accept an opportunity to negotiate that had been offered by the United States more than two years earlier, but two reasonable hypotheses have been offered.

The first holds that the Soviets, having proved that they too were a major sea power, were willing to lower the level of confrontation with the United States. And the treaty gave the Soviet Union a chance to deal with the United States as an equal. In this sense, the 1972 Incidents at Sea agreements did for the Soviets vis-à-vis the United States what the 1922 Washington Treaty did for the United States vis-à-vis Great Britain. There is some evidence supporting this hypothesis. Admiral S. G. Gorshkov, Commander in Chief of the Soviet Navy, wrote in December 1972:

> Demonstrations of naval force by the leading capitalist sea powers have been employed more than once to put pressure on the Soviet Union and the countries of the Socialist community. The U.S. Navy has especially distinguished itself by special activities in these operations. . . . Up until the signing in 1972 of the Soviet-American Incidents at Sea Treaty, there were numerous attempts at provocative clashes by American and British ships with our ships, etc. All of these actions received definite opposition on the part of the U.S.S.R. and the other Socialist countries and did not achieve those

goals at which the organizers and executioners were aiming; they merely exposed their initiators. . . .

The creation at the will of the Party of a new Soviet Navy and its emergence into the ocean expanses have fundamentally altered the relative strength of forces and the situation in this sphere of contention.[7]

A second hypothesis is at least as plausible as the first, though not as flattering to the Soviets. According to this hypothesis, senior Soviet officers were worried about the exploits of their ships. Indeed, the Soviet negotiators were astonished by the films the Americans showed them of what their ships had been doing.[8] The problem for the Soviets was to find a way to restrain their captains, such as an explicit law (Soviet officers are good at following explicit laws), but to avoid insulting them at the same time. The treaty, which on paper applied to both the U.S. Navy and the Soviet Navy equally, was just what was needed. This hypothesis also explains why the Soviets pressed for a specific distance that ships had to yield to each other; maintaining it would be like meeting the production quotas assigned to Soviet factories.

From the American viewpoint, the treaty simply reaffirmed the established Rules of the Road for navigation. If the agreement signified Soviet parity on the seas, American leaders did not admit this, and in any case, the Soviet naval buildup would have received ample publicity in the West, treaty or no treaty. It also gave the United States a channel through which to report violations to the Soviet Union; if it is true that Soviet leaders wanted the treaty in order to restrain their own captains, this would benefit both sides.

By most accounts, the Incidents at Sea Treaty has been a success. The number of near-misses and instances of harassment dropped by almost two-thirds within a year after the ratification of the agreement, and the severity of those incidents—with just a few exceptions—has also diminished. (Some exceptions include the 1983 incident in which a Soviet "Victor"-class submarine became entangled in the towed sonar gear of an American destroyer; the collision of a Soviet submarine with the aircraft carrier USS *Kitty Hawk* in March 1984 during U.S. exercises in the Sea of

Japan; and the harassment of American ships assigned to search for the wreckage of Korean Airlines Flight 007 later that same year.)

The Hot Line Agreement

Before considering just why the Incidents at Sea Treaty has been so successful, first let us consider another agreement.

By now, most people should know that the Washington-Moscow Hot Line is not a red telephone sitting on the President's desk in the White House; it is a teletype link with terminals in the Kremlin and the Pentagon. The American terminal has always been in a small anteroom of the National Military Command Center, popularly known as the War Room. (Unlike the red telephone on the President's desk, the War Room really does exist.) The terminal is manned twenty-four hours a day by military officers, among whom the Hot Line is known as the Molink, for "Moscow Link." In the early days, it was a teletypewriter of East German manufacture that looked something like a large old-fashioned typewriter housed within a polished wooden console. When the Molink was updated in the early 1970s, the East German machine was replaced by a bank of three green American-made terminals mounted side by side in racks. These machines were in turn replaced by a set of high-speed graphic printers, for reasons we will see in a moment.*

From the Pentagon, the Molink is connected to a satellite transmitting station in Frederick, Maryland, about an hour's drive from Washington. Messages can be transmitted either through the American Intelsat communications satellite or through its Soviet *Molniya* counterpart. Originally, the Hot Line was carried through transatlantic cables; the satellite links were part of the upgrade in 1971, a few years after a Norwegian farmer cut the cable line during spring plowing.

---

* The Molink staff, together with their counterparts in Moscow, test the link regularly. New Year's greetings, for example, are expected. According to staff lore, the Americans at first used the test message "The quick brown fox jumped over the lazy dog," thoroughly mystifying the Russians. For their own tests, the Soviet staff is said to favor passages from Pushkin.

• • •

The Hot Line was a direct outgrowth of the Cuban Missile Crisis, which occurred a few years after the United States and the Soviet Union had begun to deploy their first ICBMs, placing targets in each country just thirty minutes away from destruction. The SS-4 and SS-5 missiles that the Soviets deployed in Cuba would have required about a third of that time to reach their targets in the United States, as would the missiles that the United States had already deployed at (and later removed from) bases in Britain, Turkey, and Italy. A few months after the crisis, American leaders realized that some of their messages to the Soviet government had taken almost a full day to be accepted, transmitted, and acknowledged through the traditional diplomatic channels—much too slow for the missile age.

In addition, the countries had no single, dedicated link for leader-to-leader communications. (At one point the United States resorted to sending messages to the Soviet embassy via ABC correspondent John Scali, who had been approached earlier by a member of the Soviet legation.) So the Americans were uncertain whom they were actually communicating with in the Soviet Union, or who was making decisions there. The most famous example of the confusion reigning at the time of the Cuban Missile Crisis was the receipt of two messages within a few hours on October 25, 1962, both purporting to be from Premier Khrushchev—one personal and conciliatory, the other seeming very official and making a series of demands.

The Soviets never ran into the problem of receiving two contradictory messages from the White House within hours of each other. But they did have the problem of deciding which actions by American military forces or diplomats reflected the actual intentions of American leaders, and which were just the result of lower-level officials performing standard operations or acting on their own initiative. For example, at one point in the crisis an American electronic reconnaissance aircraft strayed over Soviet airspace in the Arctic. It was an Air Force pilot on a routine intelligence-gathering mission, but it could have been interpreted as the precursor to an American nuclear strike.[9]

This was unacceptable. A few months after the crisis, officials in the White House and the State Department suggested establishing a direct communications connection between Washington and Moscow. (It is difficult to determine who came up with the idea first; it had been kicking around in staff studies and in the arms control movement for some time.) The United States quickly drafted a proposal, submitted it for consideration at the ongoing eighteen-nation disarmament talks being held at Geneva, and an agreement was quickly reached in June 1963.

The original agreement stipulated that the Americans would give the Soviets four terminals for messages from the United States, and that the Soviets would give the Americans similar equipment for messages from the Soviet Union (hence the East German teletype). The original Hot Line cable stretched through Britain, Norway, Denmark, Sweden, and Finland, with a backup radio link routed through Morocco. The satellite replacement was part of a new agreement the two countries negotiated in 1971. It has since been superseded by more modern computer-based technology. The new system, adopted in 1984, cuts by two-thirds the time required to transmit written messages and makes it possible to exchange copies of charts and diagrams. (Reflecting the times, this new agreement is probably the first major Soviet-American treaty to make reference to "5¼ inch floppy disks" and "digital facsimile output with buffered random data.")[10]

The Hot Line seemed such a logical solution to the problem of rapid communication between leaders in the nuclear age that it was followed by similar links connecting the Kremlin to the Elysée Palace in Paris in 1966 and to 10 Downing Street in London in 1967. Since then, some people have suggested additional measures of this type. The best-known proposal is probably one sponsored by Senators Sam Nunn and John Warner, who would establish a joint Soviet-American crisis center. Such a center would be staffed by representatives from each side, who would be able to consult each other at a moment's notice. The staff would also have high-speed communications links to the White House, the Kremlin, the military command centers of each country, intelligence support, and so on. An agreement to discuss such a proposal was one result of the Reagan-Gorbachev meeting in Geneva in November 1985.[11]

• • •

The Hot Line was first used in 1967, when the Soviet leadership sent Lyndon Johnson a message on the first day of the June War between Israel and its Arab neighbors. The message, signed by Aleksei Kosygin, stated that the Soviet Union did not intend to intervene in the war and was willing to work with the United States to impose a cease-fire as quickly as possible. (Evidently, the Soviets had learned how badly the war had begun for the Arabs.) A few days later, the United States sent its own message, alerting the Soviet leaders that a sizable number of American aircraft and ships were being sent to the eastern end of the Mediterranean to assist the intelligence-collection ship USS *Liberty*, which had been mistakenly attacked by Israeli patrol boats; Johnson feared that the Soviets might misinterpret the movement of forces as an American intervention.

The Hot Line was used again during the 1970 war between India and Pakistan, when the United States alerted the Soviet Union of the movement of U.S. forces in the region, and in the 1973 Yom Kippur War, when the Soviets were trying to press the United States to make Israel accept a cease-fire. (By this time the messages being received from the Soviet Union were signed by Leonid Brezhnev.)[12] The most recent use of the Hot Line for anything other than testing appears to have been during the 1979 Soviet invasion of Afghanistan, when Jimmy Carter sent messages to Brezhnev protesting the airlifting of Soviet troops into Kabul, and Brezhnev sent messages to Carter indicating that the Soviets had peaceful motives.[13]

Some critics—*New York Times* columnist James Reston is one of the most visible—complain that the Hot Line is a failure because it has done little to improve overall Soviet-American relations. Critics such as Reston also complain that the line has generally been used by leaders just for posturing during crises, rather than really trying to resolve them. Worst of all, they say, pennyante treaties like the Hot Line Agreement divert attention from the lack of progress in more important areas—meaning, of course, numerical limits on nuclear weapons.

Other critics complain that the Hot Line and other arrangements to consult with the Soviets during crises are merely an invitation for Soviet deception. (The threat of deception—or, to use the Soviet term, *moskorovka*—is a favorite topic among hawkish writers these days.) One of these critics is a former Soviet KGB officer who defected to the West and now writes under the nom de plume "Viktor Suvorov." He claims that the invasion of Afghanistan was a hint of what is to come in a direct Soviet-American confrontation. Suvorov writes that even as the Soviet troops were preparing to move, Brezhnev was on the teletype lulling Carter into complacency; one can imagine what would happen if the Soviets decided to attack the United States or one of its allies directly. (Suvorov, incidentally, seems to have his story wrong; if the former President's memoirs are accurate, Carter called first and was put off by Brezhnev's blatant lies.)[14]

Whether or not the Hot Line has been a "success" depends almost entirely on what one wanted it to do. Recall the circumstances that led the two superpowers to adopt it. During the Cuban Missile Crisis, leaders on both sides were frustrated by the hours that were required to transmit a message, and sometimes the messages themselves were confusing. In other words, the problem was how to cut through the delay and confusion.

Taken on its own terms, the Hot Line did what it was supposed to do. A Hot Line message is like a Mailgram or a Federal Express letter; the channel is not used often, so when the message arrives, it stands out, and Soviet and American leaders seem to take such messages seriously. And the Hot Line does cut down on the time required to transmit messages from one country to the other.

It is only when the Hot Line Agreement is burdened with other expectations that it appears to have failed. Dovish writers expected (or at least hoped) that it would have "spillover effects"—meaning that since the Americans and Soviets had found this one enterprise in their mutual interest, perhaps they would find others. Alas, what the Hot Line may have illustrated is just how narrow the range of clearly defined mutual interests between the two countries may be. Given these expectations, it is hardly surprising that other pacts linked with détente, such as economic agreements, cultural exchanges, and joint space-exploration missions, have also "failed." Once one assumes that these treaties *ought* to lead to more significant forms of cooperation, they are bound to disappoint (and thus "fail") at some point.

Hawkish writers, who seem to believe that anything broadcast over the Hot Line ought to translate automatically into American security, also doom such agreements by overexpectation. No one ever guaranteed that a Hot Line message would be truthful or even helpful; they only promised that it would come through loud and clear and not require half a day to reach its intended audience. After that, it is up to the listener to decide whether the message is the truth, a lie, or something in between—just like any other message that a policymaker receives from an adversary.

Why the Treaties Were Successful

Why did the Incidents at Sea Treaty and the Hot Line Agreement prove so successful? First, *the agreements were practically costless*. With the possible exception of the hot-rodding Soviet naval commanders, it is difficult to think of a faction in either the Soviet or the American government that could object to the Incidents at Sea pact.* The typical destroyer or cruiser today costs in the neighborhood of $500 million to $1 billion, so avoiding collisions is probably a good idea for both parties to the treaty (not to mention the lives risked in such situations).

Similarly, the Hot Line: Leaders in both countries could see some use in having a direct link to their counterparts in the opposing country. If they did not choose to use the system, they were not compelled to do so; it was simply there if they wanted it.

Interestingly, it is precisely *because* these agreements did not cost either side much that some arms control supporters disparage them, as though the lack of cost makes them insignificant. Of course, if one expects arms control to prove that the Soviet Union and the United States can work out their disagreements peacefully, then the Incidents at Sea and Hot Line agreements

---

* Some U.S. Navy officials did worry that a specified distance to be maintained between ships would interfere with some surveillance missions. Indeed, the Navy was reluctant even to allow the subject to be discussed, as it did not want to give the Soviets any idea of the distances under which their sensors operated.

do not amount to much; the agreements are, admittedly, not significant as extraordinary examples of a "willingness to bargain in good faith" or a "spirit of compromise."

But why should progress in arms control be credited only when countries act against what leaders perceive to be their own best interest? The Incidents at Sea Treaty and Hot Line Agreement have produced real, practical benefits in enabling the superpowers to keep conflicts from escalating by accident. In the nuclear age, that is nothing to deprecate.

The second reason for the success of the two treaties was that *verification was simple.* It was easy for both countries to ascertain whether the other was keeping its commitments. A violation of the Incidents at Sea Treaty would be apparent as soon as one country's ship drifted into the other country's naval formation. Such maneuvers are difficult to cover up; there are usually too many witnesses at the scene. (The incidents that occurred before the treaty went into effect were documented by lots of photographs.) Similarly, if either side broke the Hot Line Agreement, it would be apparent as soon as the other side sent a message and no one answered.

Verification was especially important for the United States; as we have seen, it is almost entirely an American concern in arms control talks. Gathering the necessary technical evidence of violations is not the only problem; American leaders must also be able to convince a significant part of the foreign policy bureaucracy, the American public, and the public's representatives in Congress. (The same is true when U.S. officials want to make a case that the Soviets have complied with a controversial pact.)

One of the problems with the strategic arms limitation agreements up to now is that while they may have been *technically* verifiable, they were not *politically* verifiable. The American government might have had evidence suggesting that the Soviets had violated the agreement, but for one reason or another using this evidence presented problems or was ineffective.

Violations of the SALT agreements are referred to sessions of the Standing Consultative Commission (SCC), a Soviet-American body established after SALT I in order to deal with violations and alleged violations of the treaty. Soviet and American repre-

sentatives meet in the SCC, and if either country has a question
as to whether the other has violated the treaty, the evidence is
presented and the accused country either discontinues the protested action or presents evidence that it has not broken the
agreement.

Fine in theory; more difficult in practice. First, and most important, the SCC has no authority over either of the two countries; it is merely a forum for airing protests and views. If the
United States claims that the Soviets are violating the SALT II
ban on the development of more than just one new ICBM by
flight-testing two new missiles, and the Soviets assert that one
of the missiles is merely a modification of an existing ICBM,
the protest is simply left standing. The United States can either
press its claim by threatening to withdraw from the treaty—a
tactic carrying significant costs—or can walk away from the SCC
grumbling. Usually it does the latter (though the Reagan Administration did cite Soviet violations as one reason for its decision to exceed the SALT II limits on MIRVs in late 1986).

Whatever means of verification are used must also convince
the *American public* that the Soviets have not cheated, or at least
that the Soviets have not been able to gain a significant advantage with whatever cheating they have been able to get away
with. If a convincing case cannot be made, the treaty fails the
test; if convincing the public requires the government to compromise its intelligence sources excessively, again the treaty fails the
test.

Verifying the strategic arms pacts requires one to believe in
the evidence of tiny blips of electromagnetic energy detected by
receivers hundreds or thousands of miles away, and in satellite
photographs that few people (at least in theory) ever see. Some
well-informed and intelligent people may believe that the Soviets
have kept their word and complied with SALT, but that is quite
beside the point. The real question is whether enough of the
public believes in Soviet compliance for the treaty to survive
the American political system. It is readily apparent that, in at
least some cases, they do not.

A second problem with the SCC is that using it undermines
U.S. intelligence, because almost all of the information that the
United States has concerning Soviet weapons is obtained through

intelligence sources (e.g., reconnaissance satellites, radio-signal intercepts, reports from spies). So when American representatives call attention to a particular Soviet weapon or military operation, we signal the Soviets what we have been watching. Then it usually is not too difficult for them to figure out how we obtained our information. Usually the Soviet response has been to dismiss the American protest and then take countermeasures that make it more difficult for us to observe the questionable activities in the future.

For example, one of the limits included in the SALT II agreement permitted each country to develop one, and only one, ICBM. Of course, it is relatively easy to determine whether the United States is adhering to the agreement; one simply refers to *The New York Times*. Tracking the development of Soviet missiles, though, is considerably more difficult.

In the 1960s, the Soviet Union often paraded its missiles each year through Red Square during celebrations of the October Revolution. As long as our military attachés could photograph them, we could keep track of new Soviet missiles with reasonable confidence. Alas, the Soviets do not break out their ICBMs for parades anymore. Indeed, the West has not seen an unclassified photograph of a Soviet ICBM since 1969 (all of the photos of Soviet missiles that appear on the network news from time to time have been dug out of the archives). So how can the United States prove that the Soviets have developed more than one new ICBM?

This is exactly the problem that the United States faced in the early 1980s. The Soviets had been developing the SS-24, their counterpart to the MX, and officially notified the United States that this missile would be the new ICBM that they were permitted by SALT II. The SS-24 was nothing like any missile the Soviets had developed before; it was about the same size as their SS-17 and SS-19 missiles, but unlike them, the SS-24 uses solid rather than liquid fuel.

There was no chance that the Soviets could pass off the SS-24 as a modified version of the old weapons, and they did not try. Yet, according to the unanimous opinion of the U.S. intelligence community, the Soviets have also developed a second, smaller solid-propellant missile, the SS-25. The SS-25 is about half the size of the SS-24. When the United States confronted the Soviets with the SS-25 violation at the SCC, the Soviet delegates claimed that it was simply a modification of a missile deployed in 1969, the SS-13. (The SS-13 was also solid-fueled, so the story was at least plausible.)

The evidence leading the American analysts to their conclusion came from a variety of intelligence sources.[15] For the sake of illustration, though, suppose that the American delegates had presented the Soviets with photographic evidence that they had violated the treaty. The Soviets would know that we had managed to photograph a weapon that they had tried to conceal, so they would realize that they had missed some of the capabilities of our photoreconnaissance satellites. Similarly, if the American delegates had based their protest on evidence collected through telemetry intercepts, the Soviets would soon deduce which signals we had been analyzing and take steps to conceal them.

In this case, the Soviets did start encrypting almost all of the telemetry used in SS-25 testing and tested the missiles exclusively at night, trying to hide the essential characteristics of the missile from U.S. intelligence.[16] At the SCC meetings, the Soviet delegates simply denied the American claim. The Soviets went ahead with their SS-25 testing and eventually began to deploy the missile in September 1985.[17] But notice that each counterargument to a Soviet explanation of why the SS-25 was an old missile systematically revealed one more aspect of the U.S. intelligence program, making verification of arms control (and analysis of Soviet weapons in general) that much more difficult in the future.

The issue of telemetry encryption had come up before in the SALT talks when the Soviets first began such electronic scrambling in 1974. Technically, encryption was banned by Article XII of the SALT I treaty, which required both countries "not to interfere with the national technical means of verification of the other Party." The United States protested and the Soviets stopped encrypting their telemetry then. They began again in the ICBM tests they conducted in the late 1970s, however, and the Carter Administration pressed for a total ban on encryption in the SALT II talks. The Soviets balked, and rather than lose the treaty altogether, the two countries worked out an agreement according to which the Soviets said they would not encrypt any telemetry that was essential for verification.

But how can one decide whether a particular channel of telemetry would reveal significant differences between two missiles until one has analyzed the telemetry? The Soviets had constructed a Catch-22: they said that they would abstain from encrypting any channel of telemetry that the United States could show was essential for verification; but the Americans could not determine whether a channel would reveal a violation until they had analyzed it; and they could not analyze it until it was left unencrypted, which the Soviets would not do unless the Americans had shown that it was essential for verification.

To be truthful, the issue of telemetry encryption is not as pat as is suggested here. Many American observers believe that the United States can verify a strategic arms agreement to their satisfaction even without having access to Soviet missile telemetry. But this merely illustrates that verification is as much a political issue as it is a technical issue, and if an arms control agreement is going to work, it has to pass both standards.

A third reason that the Incidents at Sea and Hot Line agreements have been successful is that *they deal with practical issues on a day-to-day basis.* One reason the Incidents at Sea Treaty is not better known is that it really does not concern anyone except for captains and helmsmen on the high seas. If you do not drive ships for a living, the Rules of the Road are not on your required-reading list.

The same cannot be said about the better-known arms control treaties negotiated in recent decades. Treaties such as SALT I and SALT II were directed at least as much toward symbolism as toward limiting nuclear weapons. Practically speaking, most strategic weapons have little worth to a military planner. Strategic nuclear weapons have instead become an accounting unit in the superpower competition: an advantage in weapons means one side is ahead of the other, and a growing number of weapons indicates that the competition is heating up. So arms control agreements limiting strategic weapons are as much a game of maneuver in the unreal competition of imagery as they are limits on usable military strength.

The decisions affected by the Incidents at Sea Treaty, however, are real—concrete choices individual captains must make whenever a Soviet and an American naval ship approach each other. This "tests" the agreement frequently, and frequent testing builds confidence. In contrast, the decisions affected by the SALT agreements—arms deployment policies—are made by large organizations, elected officials, and waves of public pressure. Moreover, such decisions usually take months or years to resolve, if indeed they ever are in any permanent way. So these treaties are "tested" only on relatively rare occasions separated by long periods of time—say, during a congressional vote concerning one major weapon system or another, or in a presidential directive to begin dismantling old weapons such as Poseidon submarines so that new Trident boats can be built while still keeping the United States within the SALT limits. And these decisions are usually tied in the public's mind to such grand constructs as the "strategic balance" or simply whether the Soviet Union "is ahead" of the United States.

Finally, the negotiations for the Incidents at Sea and Hot Line agreements were conducted at a surprisingly low level in the bureaucracy, so there was little to be gained by either country in using the negotiations as a public relations event; no one in the public would know what was going on. The talks consisted of one professional talking to another about the tools of their trade; this kept the talks on course and businesslike.

The Nonproliferation Treaty

For the most part, these characteristics of successful arms control also appear in a third international agreement: the Nonproliferation Treaty, which was completed in 1968.

This is a special case of arms control. Technically, it is an agreement among the nonnuclear signatories not to acquire nuclear weapons, and among the nuclear signatories not to give nuclear weapons or nuclear weapon technology to countries that do not yet have them. In a real sense, however, the Nonproliferation Treaty is an agreement among the United States, the Soviet Union, and Great Britain to maintain an oligopoly on nuclear weapons (perhaps with the collusion of a few other countries, such as Japan, Sweden, and West Germany, which could have developed nuclear weapons but were opposed to them for ideological reasons).

Strictly speaking, the first proposal for a nonproliferation treaty was the Baruch Plan, which had been presented to the United Nations in 1947. As we have seen, however, the Baruch Plan failed for entirely logical reasons: the United States would not relinquish its nuclear weapons until it was certain that no other country would develop them, and the Soviet Union would not give up its nuclear weapons program until the United States disarmed its own nuclear forces. Both superpowers continued developing nuclear and thermonuclear weapons, with the British joining the nuclear club in 1953.

By the mid-1950s, it became clear that nuclear weapons could not be eliminated and that nuclear technology was or would eventually be within the capabilities of several countries. Furthermore, it seemed at the time that nuclear energy would produce power that was, as the saying went, "too cheap to meter," so the economic incentives for developing nuclear power appeared irresistible. Faced with these developments, American leaders had to make a choice: either curb the development of nuclear technology to the best of their ability (knowing that the effort would eventually fail) or encourage the development of nuclear power under American supervision.

The result was the "Atoms for Peace" program, announced by President Eisenhower at the United Nations in December 1953. It reversed the provisions of the McMahon Act of 1946 which prohibited the transfer of any atomic technology or nuclear materials to other countries, and it permitted American corporations to sell reactors and fissile material abroad. Also as part of the plan, in 1957 the UN established the International Atomic Energy Agency (IAEA), which was responsible for sending personnel to each reactor to make sure that it was being used for only nonmilitary purposes. Even more important, the IAEA was to account for the flow of fissile material into and out of each reactor, in order to make sure that none was diverted to make weapons. The terms of the Atoms for Peace program were generous, and the results were what one might expect: by the mid-

1960s, most European countries and a surprising number of Third World countries, such as Israel, India, Pakistan, South Africa, Iran, and Argentina, were all operating nuclear reactors.

This was troubling, however, because though the IAEA could monitor each reactor, each uranium enrichment plant, and the flow of fissile material, there was no guarantee that at some point a country would not become sufficiently independent in technology and withdraw from the international arrangement. Even with a single reactor and a limited amount of fuel, a country could produce a plutonium weapon or two each year for several years before the fuel was exhausted. Of course, if the country had its own source of uranium ore and enrichment plant, the danger was even greater.

The first country to act on this apprehension was Ireland, which introduced a resolution in the 1960 session of the UN General Assembly that would have prevented any country not then possessing nuclear weapons from developing them. The Soviet Union indicated the next year that it would support such an agreement, and though the Partial Test Ban Treaty diverted international attention for a few years, the Nonproliferation Treaty was completed and offered for acceptance by 1968.

Under the treaty, the United States, the Soviet Union, and Great Britain agreed not to transfer technology that would permit the development of nuclear weapons in other countries. The other countries signing the Nonproliferation Treaty agreed not to develop these weapons. France and China did not sign the agreement; DeGaulle and Mao Tse-tung were equally noted for their independent streaks, and neither wanted to undermine his country's infant nuclear weapons program. Even so, China has been reluctant to transfer nuclear weapons technology.

The Nonproliferation Treaty has been only marginally successful. It has not prevented the countries most able and most eager to acquire nuclear weapons from doing so. Since the agreement entered into effect, only India (a nonsignatory) has been detected testing a nuclear device. Israel (also a nonsignatory) has probably developed nuclear weapons as well, and South Africa and Pakistan (both nonsignatories) are waiting in the wings. This is not a remarkable record, though it is well below the rate some experts in the 1960s were predicting for nuclear proliferation.

The mechanical technology of nuclear weapons is simple enough that the decision to build a bomb usually depends more on economics than on knowledge; assuming a country has access to fissile material and is willing "to eat grass if necessary" (to quote former Pakistani leader Zulkifar Ali Bhutto), it can eventually make at least some kind of nuclear weapon. So one should not have expected that the Nonproliferation Treaty alone would prevent countries from "going nuclear." In fact, if history is an accurate predictor, countries intent on building nuclear weapons simply do not sign the treaty.

But the treaty can be viewed as more of a success when regarded mainly as a Soviet-American treaty (with a few other participants). It has allowed the inevitable spread of nuclear weapons to take place under superpower supervision; without it, many countries would have had the ability to assemble nuclear weapons on short notice. The Nonproliferation Treaty makes sense from the American and Soviet perspectives because it is bad enough to face a superpower possessing nuclear weapons without having to worry about a dozen other countries with the ability to kill millions of people. Thus, despite the Soviet-American rivalry, both superpowers find their interests best served if nuclear weapons are kept within the oligopoly as much as possible. Ford and GM probably do not like having to compete with each other, but were it not for the Sherman Act, they would not mind working together to squeeze out Chrysler. Indeed, much of the success of the Nonproliferation Treaty results from the willingness of the major nuclear powers to pressure or to bribe other countries—especially their allies—not to develop nuclear weapons.

Notice that when viewed as a big-brother agreement, the Nonproliferation Treaty has most of the characteristics for success that the Incidents at Sea and the Hot Line agreements exhibit. Neither of the two major signatories gives up much. (The other participants are coerced and enticed to share a similar perception.) The treaty is uncomplicated (though, admittedly, the policing procedures for the flow of fissile material can be somewhat tricky to administer), and most significant violations would be readily observable. Indeed, the Nonproliferation Treaty may be the only agreement in the world community today that has the combined efforts of the U.S. and Soviet intelligence communities working in its behalf. It was the Soviets, for example, who alerted the United States about the possibility that South Africa may have been developing a fission device.

Together, these three agreements—the Incidents at Sea Treaty, the Hot Line Agreement, and the Nonproliferation Treaty—probably account for the vast share of whatever success arms control can claim. The lesson seems to be that arms control, when drafted with the constraints of the real world in mind, can work. What is more, it can produce real benefits—fewer provocations on the high seas, better communication in crises, perhaps a lower rate of proliferation than might otherwise occur. Half the problem in arms control is understanding which agreements can work. The other half is to understand which cannot.

CHAPTER NINE

Some Examples of Reasonable Limits

WHEN the arms control debate began to focus on the Reagan Administration's Strategic Defense Initiative ("Star Wars") in 1984 and 1985, one of the weapons that came under scrutiny was the ASAT, or antisatellite weapon. As we saw earlier, both the United States and the Soviet Union had been testing various kinds of ASATs by 1980. And banning ASATs has become the focus of recent Soviet arms control efforts, as well as of many arms control supporters in the West.

The ASAT controversy is a good illustration of the broader issue of how arms control should fit into American national security policy. It also illustrates the limits of arms control: how it can be a poorly designed, counterproductive agreement that will fail to control arms and will increase tension between the two superpowers, or an agreement that will enhance deterrence and national security.

One problem of truly controlling ASATs was noted in Chapter Six. Banning ASATs would ban many civilian uses of space—e.g., the space shuttle, which can snatch satellites out of orbit and bring them back to earth. Yet there are other problems, which become clear once one understands the genealogy of antisatellite weapons.

ASATs are not new. The U.S. ASAT program began soon after the satellite program. Paul Stares, a research associate at the

Brookings Institution who has studied the history of ASATs, believes that proposals for antisatellite weapons resulted in large part from the American intelligence community's program to build photoreconnaissance satellites. Although some U.S. officials believed that the Soviets would not object to satellite reconnaissance (after all, it was the Soviets who had established the precedent of orbiting satellites over enemy territory when they launched *Sputnik I*), others were not so sure; the Soviets had shot down Gary Powers, and if able, they might try to interfere with U.S. satellites, too. Hence, one rationale for the ASAT was that it would persuade the Soviet Union to leave U.S. satellites alone.[1]

Another reason was the fear that the Soviet Union would deploy nuclear weapons in space. In the late 1950s, ballistic missiles were still somewhat exotic; almost all strategic forces consisted of manned bombers. Though some experts could see that these would probably be replaced or supplemented at some point in the future, there were a number of alternatives that seemed at least as plausible as ballistic missiles.

One was satellites. After all, if there could be ballistic missiles fired like artillery from halfway around the world, and pilotless cruise missiles designed to fly across the ocean, then why not satellites parked in orbit with nuclear warheads, ready to be dropped on the United States in the event of war? American officials could not dismiss the possibility that the Soviets would develop a space bombardment system, and so the United States needed some method of inspecting (and, if necessary, destroying) it.

According to Stares, the first serious proposal for a U.S. antisatellite weapon was Project SAINT, proposed by the Radio Corporation of America to the Air Force in August 1959—less than two years after Sputnik and a little over a year after the first American satellite, *Explorer I*. SAINT was mainly supposed to be a satellite inspection system (hence the name, "*Satellite Inspector*"), but American aerospace designers and officials knew that anything that could approach close enough to inspect a satellite in orbit could probably destroy it, too. But Project SAINT died in 1962, partly because civilian officials in the Defense Department such as Herbert York and Robert McNamara feared that a U.S. ASAT would simply provoke the Soviets to develop their own, partly because the Air Force had other priorities, and partly because the particular design being considered probably would not have worked anyway.[2]

The United States did develop two other projects into workable ASAT systems, however. The first was the Army's antiballistic missile system, the Nike Zeus. The United States had exploded nuclear warheads at high altitudes in tests during the early 1960s. (One of these tests, Starfish Prime, detonated a 1.4-megaton warhead at a height of 248 miles.)[3] These tests suggested that the X-rays and high-energy particles released from such explosions, meeting little resistance from the atmosphere, could fry the electronic components of all satellites within several hundred miles. So the Nike Zeus, designed to destroy incoming warheads with a megaton warhead, was readily adapted for use against satellites. The Army tested the system, developed as Project MUDFLAP, in 1962 and 1963, and the ASAT was declared operational the following year at Johnston Island in the Pacific Ocean. It was taken down two years later, mainly because it intruded on turf that had been assigned to the Air Force.[4]

The Air Force, meanwhile, was developing its own antisatellite weapon. As a result of the compromise that Kennedy and Khrushchev worked out in the Cuban Missile Crisis, the United States had removed its Thor intermediate-range ballistic missiles from Turkey, so the Air Force was left with a number of IRBMs on its hands. Since the Kennedy Administration had directed the services to develop ASATs, it made sense for the Air Force to convert them. The Air Force tested the Thor missiles against targets in space beginning in February 1964, also from Johnston Island. This system was declared operational in just five months, and the Thor remained officially deployed as an ASAT until as late as 1975. The reason for discontinuing the ASAT seems to have been that U.S. officials feared the weapon would destroy not only its Soviet target but also all American satellites within a wide area. In any case, using the Thor ASAT would have meant that the United States was crossing the "nuclear firebreak," and U.S. officials were trying at the time to reduce their need to rely on nuclear weapons.[5]

After these early ASAT programs were killed, the United States began to search for nonnuclear antisatellite systems. A few ideas had lain dormant in the technological bureaucracy for several years. One of these ideas eventually formed the basis of the "tomato can" that the United States successfully tested in 1985. The MV (maneuvering vehicle) was based on ideas originally developed for the American antiballistic program. (This is a key reason that arms control advocates oppose ASATs. The technology necessary to detect, track, and destroy satellites is nearly identical with that required to detect, track, and destroy incoming ballistic missiles; if anything, ASAT technology is simpler than ABM technology because antisatellite systems usually have to deal with fewer targets. So supporters of arms control fear that if the United States builds an ASAT, an ABM program will inevitably follow.) The MV system was developed under extraordinary secrecy during the first half of the 1970s, and was accelerated after the Soviet Union restarted its ASAT program in the middle of the decade.

It is important to understand the American ASAT program and how quickly it progressed, because the Soviet Union has developed parallel programs. The Soviet antisatellite weapon that receives the most attention today, the co-orbital system, resembles the old U.S. Thor system. The most important difference is that it uses a conventional rather than a nuclear warhead. Also, rather than using an intermediate-range missile like the Thor for the booster, the Soviet ASAT uses a booster based on the SS-9 intercontinental ballistic missile, probably because the weapon is so much heavier. The Soviet system seems to have been first tested in October 1968, though it is difficult to determine, as its existence was discovered only after Soviet satellites in the *Kosmos* series began to disappear on Western tracking systems. (The Soviets have never officially acknowledged this system, and only recently admitted to testing any ASATs at all.)

This is usually the only Soviet ASAT discussed in the West during arms control debates. Yet there are others.

Unlike the United States, the Soviets did not dismantle the anti-ballistic missile system permitted under the provisions of SALT. So they can use their GALOSH ABM interceptors in a

"MUDFLAP mode"—launching the missile into a high, lofted trajectory, in which it could attack U.S. satellites.[6]

The Soviets also appear to have two other systems. One is the high-energy laser tested at Sary Shagan. A ground-based laser, it is probably not powerful enough today to destroy a satellite in orbit, but it could burn out the delicate sensors on which many of these satellites depend.[7]

The other Soviet ASAT "system" is the network of satellite dishes scattered across the Soviet Union and its allies. If equipped with a transmitter of sufficient power, these dishes theoretically could be used to overload the circuitry of a satellite (this is called "RF burnout," referring to the radio frequencies used in the technique). The construction of such circuit-busting transmitters would probably be detected (since the Soviets would have to link them to a very large power source), and to date there have been no public reports of such projects in the Soviet Union. Moreover, the Soviets would run the risk of ruining their own satellites if they were to use such a system. But Soviets could simply use any of their existing satellite transmitters to jam communications to and from U.S. satellites.

The point is that all of these Soviet antisatellite systems exist *today*. If the Soviet Union and the United States were to face each other in a shooting conflict *today*, it is likely American military officials would see some of their low-flying reconnaissance satellites disappear and communications with the higher-flying satellites jammed.

It would be difficult to eliminate these weapons through an arms control agreement. The means necessary to assure the United States that the Soviets had indeed dismantled their co-orbital ASAT system would cause major disruptions in the Soviet space program. The Soviets have offered to dismantle their ASAT facility at Tyuratam. But the ASAT device is relatively small and could easily be hidden, and the Soviets use the same SS-9–based booster associated with their ASAT to launch two kinds of intelligence satellites; if they continued to operate these satellites, they would need to have the booster, and this booster could easily be used to launch any ASAT devices the Soviets may have saved. Therefore, any measure that would convince

U.S. officials that the co-orbital ASAT was no longer operational would most likely also deprive the Soviets of the use of these satellites—each of which probably represents an investment of several billion dollars.*

Moreover, the Soviets use another SS-9–based booster to launch military satellites from their space center to the north at Plesetsk. Theoretically, this booster could also be used to operate the co-orbital ASAT. Therefore, some U.S. officials might not be convinced that the co-orbital ASAT had truly been taken out of operation unless the facilities for this booster were dismantled, too. This would raise the costs to the Soviets even further.

The problems do not stop there. Certainly the Soviets are not going to dismantle their ABM system (which also cost the equivalent of several billion dollars and is currently being modernized) simply for the sake of an ASAT treaty. The same is true of their satellite dishes. Indeed, the technology needed to jam a satellite is virtually the same as that used to transmit commands to a satellite, so one has to wonder how feasible it is to eliminate this kind of ASAT threat.

Worse still, we sometimes forget that "Star Wars" could take place above the earth at an altitude of just 100 miles, the orbital height of a typical photoreconnaissance satellite—or about the distance from Philadelphia to New York City. This is within the range of several modern antiaircraft missiles. Just as an antiaircraft missile can be converted into an antimissile missile, and an antimissile missile can be converted into an antisatellite missile, at some point an antiaircraft missile can be converted into an antisatellite missile. And after all of these possibilities, there is still the space shuttle and its manipulator arm.

The upshot is that an outright ban on ASAT is simply not possible, and even more important, it is not a solution to the threat posed to stable deterrence by ASATs. This is the same conclusion

---

* One of these is called an "electronic ocean reconnaissance satellite," or "EORSAT"; the other is called a "radar ocean reconnaissance satellite," or "RORSAT." As their names imply, they are used by the Soviets to locate U.S. ships at sea. The Soviets seem especially concerned about our aircraft carriers. The Soviet nuclear-powered RORSAT gained notoriety in 1978 when one crashed in northern Alberta, spewing radioactive debris across the Canadian countryside.

a team of experts at the Office of Technology Assessment reached when it was directed to study this problem by the U.S. Congress. The OTA study did conclude that arms control has a role to play in dealing with the Soviet antisatellite threat; yet it also concluded that arms control alone would not suffice, as controls "cannot guarantee the survival of U.S. satellites attacked by residual or covert Soviet ASAT weapons."[8]

So is there an alternative?

The OTA study illustrated a comprehensive *system* of American policies to attack the problem. (By charter, OTA is not allowed to make policy recommendations.) Part of the plan was for the United States and the Soviet Union to agree in a treaty not to interfere with each other's satellites—a sort of Incidents at Sea Treaty for space. But because a no-interference-with-satellites treaty between the United States and the Soviet Union would not be enough (the Soviets would have the capability and incentive to violate the agreement), the OTA plan also included several other important elements.

The first was for the United States to reduce much of its dependence on satellite systems. In a little under twenty years, the U.S. military has become firmly tied to satellites for communications, reconnaissance, navigation, detection of nuclear explosions, etc. In most cases, when a satellite-based system was developed, the armed forces either discarded the previous system or allowed it to atrophy. For instance, when satellite communications became routinely available, cable-based systems were cut back.

The usual advantages satellite systems offered were efficiency or performance. (Reconnaissance satellites can go where reconnaissance aircraft cannot, for example, and satellite communications systems do not require laying cables.) However, satellite systems are not as "survivable" as some of the older technologies. Keeping both the older systems and the satellite systems in service would have cost more money and, in a world of limited budgets, may have meant sacrificing some other military assets. But the redundancy would have been good insurance against ASAT threats. The Soviets, who seem to keep all of their old military equipment, have realized this and thus maintain their older cable and high-frequency radio systems for precisely this reason.

A second element in the OTA study was how to make U.S.

satellites less vulnerable to ASAT attack. One method would be to improve their evasion capabilities, mainly by increasing the amount of fuel they carry, so they can make a great number of "dodge" maneuvers in orbit during their lifetime. (Unfortunately, more fuel also means more weight, which requires one to use a larger booster to put the satellite into space.)

Another way to reduce vulnerability would be to equip satellites with shielding or armor so that they could bounce back from pellet attacks by the Soviet co-orbital ASAT or lasers from Sary Shagan. Again, this means increasing the weight of the satellite; and in any case, there is a limit to the amount of shielding one can place on a satellite because openings have to be left for antennae, sensors, solar panels, and the like. (The same problems would apply to making a satellite less detectable by an ASAT's tracking system; any coating for camouflaging a satellite would also make it more difficult to cool, and this would reduce the efficiency of its sensors and other electronic systems.)[9]

A third way to reduce vulnerability would be to put decoys into orbit with each satellite. The main problem here is that the decoy must resemble the real satellite as closely as possible in appearance, radio emissions, heat signature—all of the features that an ASAT system might use to distinguish a real satellite from a fake. At some point simulation would cost so much that it would make sense simply to launch two satellites rather than a satellite and a decoy. (In fact, the ultimate decoy is a backup satellite.)

All of these measures are aimed at a common goal: making the prospects of a successful attack on U.S. satellites seem so small to the Soviets that they decide not to try.

Finally, OTA suggested one last countermeasure: the development of some form of American ASAT capability. The object here, of course, would be to threaten retaliation. Simply building an American ASAT would probably not be enough to deter the Soviets as things stand now, because the United States depends more on its satellites than the Soviets do on theirs. However, if the United States improved the survivability of its satellites and decreased its dependence on them, the prospects of mutual ASAT combat could begin to appear so poor to the Soviets that they would leave our satellites alone.

The ASAT lesson shows the limits of arms control. It also illustrates some alternatives to arms control and, most important, how arms control makes sense when (and only when) it is tied into the rest of U.S. national security policy.

Reasonable Limits and the Case for Unilateral Measures

The goals of the arms control lobby are straightforward—reducing the probability of war and decreasing the expense of the arms race—and few people would argue with the virtue of these goals. Unfortunately, the supporters of arms control focus their attention on traditional SALT-style ceilings and test bans, without asking whether these are really the best ways to achieve these goals.

The payoff of perfect arms control would be great; the probability of achieving it is very, very slim. And as we have seen, the probability of achieving it in the future is becoming smaller and smaller.

Some of the best steps the United States could take to avert nuclear war are unilateral measures such as improving the credibility of U.S. retaliation; reducing the incentives for the Soviet Union to strike the United States; and declaring policies that will reduce confusion and uncertainty in war.

Improving Command and Control. Recall the study that Albert Wohlstetter conducted at Rand on the vulnerability of SAC bomber bases. Wohlstetter understood that deterrence depended on retaliation, which required SAC forces to clear several discrete hurdles. First, they had to survive a Soviet strike, by escaping from their bases or by riding out the attack in shelters. Second, they had to receive a command to retaliate and instructions how to do so. Third, they had to penetrate Soviet defenses and reach their targets. Fourth, they had to overcome Soviet passive defenses, such as civil defense. If the likelihood that SAC would fail to clear *any one* of these hurdles equaled zero—say, if the command and control system were destroyed and the order to retaliate could not be communicated to the forces—then the probability of retaliation would also equal zero. This would make deterrence precarious indeed, which is why Wohlstetter called the situation the "Delicate Balance of Terror."[10]

Yet, how secure is U.S. command and control? Most experts today believe that the answer is "not nearly as secure as it should be." Bruce Blair, for example, has recently written one of the most comprehensive studies of the problem.[11] While most people have studied the vulnerability of U.S. strategic missiles and bombers to a preemptive Soviet attack, Blair argues that the more pressing threat is the vulnerability not of the weapons themselves but rather of the communications system necessary to operate them. He is especially concerned with the "nodes" (critical choke points, such as ICBM launch control centers or SAC headquarters) in the communications network.

The Soviet Union has deployed about 7,000 strategic nuclear warheads on various kinds of missiles, submarines, and bombers. The Soviets might be able to destroy almost all of the 2,000 or so warheads that the United States has on its Minuteman missiles, but it would be impossible for them to destroy the remaining 8,000-odd weapons on U.S. bombers and submarines. So it would seem U.S. retaliatory forces are secure. Yet, according to Blair, the U.S. command and control system necessary to operate these forces could be thoroughly obliterated by an attack on just 400 communications nodes; even a well-coordinated attack on fifteen key facilities would cause much disruption. All scenarios of strategic nuclear war contain a good amount of unreality, but if nuclear deterrence *can* break down (and this is a central assumption of the argument for arms control), then those fifteen command and control centers should be made less vulnerable, or less vital to the ability of the United States to launch a retaliatory strike.

In addition to the earthbound command and control system, the United States also has a backup system of airborne command posts. The assumption is that the Soviets would be unable to destroy aircraft flying random patterns over the United States. One of these planes, code-named "Looking Glass," is a backup for Strategic Air Command Headquarters that is kept aloft at all times. However, as Blair points out, SAC Headquarters is only the most obvious link in the chain, and other command posts in the system are not kept on airborne alert.

Moreover, any airborne command post can remain aloft for only a limited period of time; they can be refueled, but eventually their engines run out of oil and fail. Hence, if for some reason the instructions for retaliation are not completed within the lifetime of the engines, the command and control network would begin to break down. Blair also identifies other weak links, such as the vulnerability of the launch control centers for U.S. ICBMs and the vulnerability of our early-warning radars to attack or sabotage.

There are solutions: instead of relying on aircraft as backup command posts, for example, U.S. forces could use mobile command posts based in trucks or trains. Most of the technology already exists, and the entire mobile system might cost $10 billion—a sizable amount of money, but compare the value of this investment for strengthening deterrence with what the United States currently spends on the strategic weapons that the command and control system is supposed to operate.

Moreover, compare the contribution such an expenditure would make to stable deterrence with what would have been achieved by recent proposals for arms control. Suppose, for example, the United States and the Soviet Union adopted the basic guidelines of the START proposals that were on the negotiating table at the end of 1986. (Though the U.S. and Soviet proposals differed on some details and the SDI question, both were based on the general principle of making deep cuts in strategic weapons.) The United States would have continued its modernization program for strategic nuclear forces to the extent allowed by the treaty. When done, the United States would have spent about $20 billion on new weapons and would have reduced the number of strategic warheads it deployed to 6,000—about half of what it deploys today. Soviet forces would be cut to similar levels.

Would war be more likely with a START treaty—leaving a "few" thousand warheads on each side, and at least one side having a fragile command and control system—or with no START treaty, about twice as many warheads, but also a secure command and control system? At least in this case, it would seem that deterrence would be more reliable without arms control, simply because what the United States did with its own forces would dominate the entire situation; arms control is a minor factor.

Reducing the Number of Targets. During the 1970s, the Soviet Union developed a new generation of ICBMs: the SS-16 (which was effectively banned by SALT II), the SS-17 (which never appeared to work very well), and (most important for our purposes here) the SS-18 and SS-19. Unlike all previous Soviet intercontinental missiles, the SS-18 and SS-19 were both "MIRVed" (equipped with multiple warheads) *and* were both incredibly accurate, easily on a par with any similar weapon that the United States had deployed. According to U.S. intelligence, if the Soviets were to aim at a target with their SS-18s or SS-19s, they could be certain that half of the warheads would land within a 1,000- to 1,600-foot circle around the target. So for the first time, the Soviets had a large number of weapons with the yield and accuracy to destroy a hardened target such as an American Minuteman silo or a launch control bunker.

The Soviets had deployed "silo-busters" before. Some versions of the SS-9, for example, carried a 20-megaton warhead, which would easily destroy a silo. However, the SS-9 was large and expensive, and each SS-9 could carry only one 20-megaton warhead. Therefore, the Soviets could never endanger the U.S. ICBM force with it (though there was a good chance they could have destroyed most of the launch control centers necessary for firing them off). The accuracy of the new missiles meant that the Soviets could use a smaller warhead to threaten the same target; two 350–500-kiloton warheads fired from the new ICBMs had about a nine-out-of-ten chance of destroying their target. Since it was now practical for the Soviets to pack several "hard-target kill" warheads on each SS-18 (which carried ten) and SS-19 (which carried six), they could threaten the large number of U.S. ICBM silos with a relatively small number of missiles. The Soviets deployed 308 SS-18s and 360 SS-19s. This theoretically gave the Soviets 5,240 warheads capable of destroying Minuteman silos. (The intelligence community reassessed the SS-19's accuracy in 1986 and determined that the missile was less threatening than originally thought, but this did not change the basic argument concerning the vulnerability of the Minuteman force.)

The response of the arms control supporters, naturally, was to oppose the program for modernizing U.S. strategic forces (which included the MX missile, intended to provide the United States with its own high-accuracy warheads to threaten Soviet ICBM silos) and to advocate arms control as a means to reduce the number of Soviet ICBMs. Yet a much more logical solution was something the United States could have done entirely on its own, without the difficulties and years of delay that negotiating an arms control treaty would have produced: simply eliminate the Minuteman force, digging the silos out of the ground and replacing them with mobile ICBMs and submarine-launched missiles. This unilateral measure probably would have done more to diminish the odds of nuclear war than any formal arms control agreement likely to be feasible in the foreseeable future. *

One can attack the vulnerability problem either through arms control or through unilateral measures. The chief advantage of unilateral measures is that they are much more easily adopted, meaning that they are much more likely to *be* adopted. Assuming the SS-18 system costs about as much as the MX system the United States is deploying, any arms control treaty that had the Soviets scrap their SS-18 force would cost them $30–$40 billion (actually more, as the SS-18 force is at least three times as large as any MX system will ever be) and thirty years of heavy ICBM development. On top of that, the Soviet Union would have to ensure that the United States could monitor the agreement to the satisfaction of the American political system. One can imagine the difficulties any Soviet leader would have in justifying this to his colleagues. The unilateral alternative, on the other hand,

* Three caveats:

First, some analysts might have objected to this plan because submarine-launched missiles have lacked the accuracy to destroy Soviet ICBM silos and leadership shelters. This will no longer be true once the planned D-5 missile is deployed on Trident submarines, so if one wants to target such facilities, submarine-launched missiles could be used, as could a mobile ICBM.

Second, other individuals, such as Senator Pete Wilson of California, would have criticized mobile missiles as being an expensive, inefficient way to deliver a warhead; the proposed Small ICBM, for example, will probably carry one warhead (perhaps two), while the MX will carry ten. This is true, but the added cost is the price of reducing vulnerability.

Finally, all of this assumes that the United States also improves the survivability of its command and control systems. If they were not made mobile or concealable, the Soviets would have the same incentive to strike them as they would have to strike the weapons themselves.

would require the passage of a number of expensive bills through Congress. This is no simple task, but certainly it must be easier to shape the policies of one country than of two.

The desire of many arms control supporters for an international agreement borders on a fetish. Why should a country devote so much of its manpower, political capital, and public debate to an arms control solution to problems that could be solved much more easily by other means?

Arms control enjoys a rare place among the activities undertaken by the U.S. government. No policy analyst would recommend building a tunnel underneath a river without first studying whether a bridge might be cheaper. No defense official would propose building a 90,000-ton aircraft carrier without at least being prepared to show why it is a better buy than a 60,000-ton alternative. We expect comparisons, at least in principle. But arms control is a policy favored by most government officials purely for its own sake.

No First Use. One last alternative is attractive because it could be packaged to look like traditional forms of arms control.

At about the same time the nuclear freeze movement was heating up (so to speak), another movement was under way, also in reaction to the threat of nuclear war. This was the movement that favored the adoption by the United States of a "no first use," or "NFU," policy. The United States was to announce that it would use nuclear weapons only in retaliation for a nuclear attack on itself or its allies. If no other country used nuclear weapons, then the United States would not, either.

The Soviets favored "no first use" because it fit into propaganda that they had been using for many years. Because the Warsaw Pact enjoys a decisive edge over NATO in the number of conventional forces on the Central Front of Europe and in the speed at which these forces can get to battle, NFU works to the Pact's favor. If a European war can be kept from going nuclear, the Soviet Union and its allies would most likely win, at a price far below what it would be if nuclear weapons were used.

This also explains the official reluctance of the United States to accept "no first use." NATO's dependence on nuclear weapons dates from the very beginnings of the alliance. In 1952, NATO members met at Lisbon to consider the military requirements for defending the alliance from a Soviet attack. The estimate, which came to be called the Lisbon Force Requirements, was so clearly beyond the means of the members—the Europeans were still recovering from World War II—that NATO quickly shifted to a nuclear strategy. Not only would the alliance rely on the nuclear-armed artillery and short-range missiles that had just been developed; NATO war plans, especially in the early days, called for the United States to hit the Soviet Union with an all-out strategic nuclear strike. (Indeed, during the 1950s, most attack plans would have taken out eastern Europe and China as well.) Once the Soviet Union developed its own nuclear weapons, any U.S. threat to use nuclear weapons became less and less credible. But NATO continues to use the nuclear threat because the conventional forces needed to defend it against a Soviet attack have been no more forthcoming in the 1980s than in the 1950s.

Still, the "no first use" movement enjoyed broad support. The antinuclear lobby favored it, of course. However, NFU also received the implicit endorsement of a number of military officials. For example, John Hackett, the former commander of the Northern Group of Forces on NATO's Central Front (and author of *The Third World War,* a story predicting how a war between the Warsaw Pact and NATO would unfold in the mid-1980s), was one "supporter." He believed that any threat by NATO to use nuclear weapons was so obviously bogus that the alliance had in effect already adopted a "no first use" policy. All that remained, said Hackett, was for the alliance to supply the conventional forces that such a policy—the de facto policy then in effect—required.

Even General Bernard Rogers, former Supreme Allied Commander in Europe, criticized deterring conventional forces with nuclear weapons. (Rogers also criticized U.S. efforts to cut the overall number of nuclear weapons in NATO.) Rogers pointed out the problems entailed in NATO's nuclear threat and claimed that the forces needed for a conventional defense, if properly selected, were affordable. He favored using advanced-technology, high-accuracy nonnuclear weapons against Warsaw Pact forces before they arrived at the front.

Not only does the threat of Soviet retaliation make NATO's nuclear deterrent unconvincing; it is difficult to think of any way in which nuclear weapons, even if used, would enable NATO to win a war. When NATO leaders assert they need nuclear weapons to defend the Central Front, usually they talk about the Warsaw Pact's advantage in conventional forces and NATO's inability to fund the men and weapons necessary to overcome it. But they rarely explain how nuclear weapons solve the problem.

Not only would a good portion of western Europe be destroyed in any nuclear war; the Soviets are also better prepared to fight a nuclear war at almost any level of escalation. The Warsaw Pact is more highly mechanized, it trains more often for fighting in a "nuclear environment," it relies less on the high-technology military electronics that would probably fail once nuclear weapons were used, and so on. Nuclear weapons may be NATO's answer to the Warsaw Pact's advantage in conventional forces, but they are not the solution.

Hackett is almost certainly correct. The odds of a war on the Central Front are admittedly not large, but if deterrence in Europe ever hinges decisively on nuclear weapons, it would probably fail because the Soviets would not believe NATO's nuclear threat. But the nuclear guarantee is not only a failure; it is positively dangerous. Because there is at least *some* possibility that NATO will resort to nuclear warfare, the Soviets have an incentive to strike first with nuclear weapons, if only to destroy NATO's nuclear forces. There is also the hazard that the NATO chain of command will be short-circuited, leading to a 15-kiloton mistake somewhere in West Germany.

The only reasonable justification for deploying nuclear weapons in Europe today is to deter the Soviets from using their own nuclear weapons. But this point should be made clear, and a policy of NFU would help prevent miscalculation or mistakes. It might also make sense as a political lever to acquire the conventional forces NATO needs.

Although the United States could declare "no first use" unilaterally, it also could use the issue to its advantage as part of an "arms control" agreement, jointly announced with the Soviet Union. "No first use" is simple to monitor and enforce, much like the Incidents at Sea Treaty: any violations are self-evident, and compliance is a function of deterrence. Even under an NFU policy, NATO would retain some nuclear weapons and could retaliate against a Soviet nuclear attack.

NFU, in fact, is only one type of agreement that follows this form. Others are possible, such as a "no first use against cities" policy. As terrible as any nuclear attack would be, a concentrated strike against cities would be especially horrible. Not only would millions of noncombatants be immediately killed, chemical plants and factories would burn, poisoning the atmosphere and resulting in even more casualties. (The "nuclear winter" thesis, which holds that almost any nuclear war would lead to a fall in global temperatures and kill most life on Earth, is far from proven, but the general principle of the environmental hazards of nuclear war seems valid.) The same is true of attacks on nuclear reactors; consider the catastrophe that the meltdown at Chernobyl caused, and recall that there are about 200 nuclear reactors that can be targeted in the United States alone. So treaties providing for "no first use against cities" and "no first use against reactors" might someday prove their worth.

This approach to arms control is admittedly less ambitious than most current proposals, including those now being presented by the Soviet Union and the United States. About the only thing going for it is that it is feasible and not counterproductive.

CHAPTER **TEN**

A Strategy for Arms Control

THIS book is not an indictment of arms control, but of how it has been pursued up to now. Arms control agreements can improve U.S. security and reduce the potential for war, but only if we understand its limitations as well as its potential. If arms control has been less than a success up to now, it is in large part because these limitations have been ignored.

First, *arms control is not an end in itself.* Frequently one hears that "Soviet-American relations will improve if an accommodation on arms control can be reached." Sometimes one reads a newspaper columnist wondering when the United States will make progress in arms control, as though the State Department were a factory that had to meet a quota for treaties.

This is sloppy thinking. Arms control is a means, not an end. It makes no more sense to ask why the government has not produced more arms control treaties than to ask why the government has not produced more laws. Each treaty must be judged on what it accomplishes, not whether it is successfully negotiated.

Similarly, arms control treaties do not necessarily guarantee improved relations between the Soviet Union and the United States. Some may, but some can increase rather than reduce tension. Other treaties may have no effect at all. Besides, the belief that arms control will improve Soviet-American relations confuses cause and effect. Arms control agreements that require the United States or the Soviet Union to give up some weapons

194

program deemed essential to security—for the United States space-based defenses or for the Soviet Union heavy ICBMs—are by-products of stable Soviet-American relations. They require super-power relations to improve *before* they can be made.

By itself, "improving superpower relations" is a poor reason for arms control. An agreement must have specific objectives; otherwise, it is impossible to determine whether it is in the national interest. For example, if the goal of the United States is to ensure that its satellites will not be destroyed by the Soviet Union in a war or in a crisis, a ban on antisatellite weapons is not the way to achieve the goal; an ASAT ban would not pro-tect U.S. satellites. It makes much more sense for the United States to deploy some type of antisatellite weapon in order to de-ter the Soviet Union from attacking U.S. satellites, and then clarify the understanding between the two countries that inter-fering with the functions of orbital satellites is prohibited.

Indeed, if no one bothers to define the specific objectives of an arms control agreement, it is impossible to determine whether they are even feasible. Suppose, for example, that the United States wants to reduce U.S. defense spending. Logic and three-quarters of a century of evidence suggest that arms control can-not achieve this objective; in fact, an agreement intended to re-duce U.S. defense expenditures may make them rise.

Although one must accept that not every arms control negotia-tion will succeed, the negotiations themselves do not seem to hurt. Talks between the Soviet Union and the United States dur-ing the past decade and a half have probably improved each side's understanding of the other. Also, if an arms control agree-ment is worth negotiating, it is better to have a forum for talk-ing already in existence, so that the decision to meet is not it-self a major hurdle. (This is also why it is a good idea to have regular meetings between Soviet and American officials at vari-ous levels in the government—the American President and the So-viet General Secretary, the U.S. Secretary of Defense and the Soviet Defense Minister, the Chief of Naval Operations and the Commander in Chief of the Soviet Navy, and so on.)

Second, *bad arms control is worse than no arms control at all.* Supporters of arms control have rarely been critical of any agree-ment that appears to limit weapons. This has been a mistake.

Nothing prevents a country from accepting an arms control agreement that will, in the end, increase its defense costs and reduce its security. Bad agreements not only do direct harm, they also discredit arms control as a whole.

Third, *arms control that depends on retarding technology will fail.* Countries can try to stall military technology. They might even be able to negotiate an agreement banning the development of certain weapons. However, there are just too many alternative ways to develop the technology eventually used for weapons. It is difficult even to anticipate, let alone control, them. And, in any case, the effective banning of military technology, such as tanks, bombers, and guncotton, would be impossible without eliminating many civilian technologies, such as tractors, airliners, and synthetic fertilizer.

Fourth, *in negotiating arms control, success does not necessarily lead to success; one arms control agreement can actually limit the feasibility of future agreements.* Since a successful arms control agreement can spur the development of weapons that are more difficult to count or monitor, the second round of arms control talks may be more difficult than the first. Also, though developments in technology may open new opportunities for arms control (as with the development of reconnaissance satellites), other developments may just as quickly limit such opportunities (as with the development of small, highly mobile cruise missiles that are difficult to locate with reconnaissance satellites). Arms control is best directed at arms whose control is feasible.

Fifth, *unilateral policies that accomplish the same objectives as arms control are usually better.* Changing government policies that are based on billion-dollar weapon systems and involve the very security of a nation is like changing the course of a supertanker. But it is easier to change the course of one supertanker than two.

And, sixth, *if an arms control agreement is to be negotiated, it is best negotiated quietly among a small group of representatives from each country.* Quiet diplomacy allows flexibility and the ability to ignore the continual advice of Congress and the bureaucracy. Such freedom is probably necessary to negotiate an agreement affecting any major weapons system.

The usual objection to "quiet diplomacy" is that it is undemocratic and that it fails to represent the "true wishes" of the American people. This objection, though, is not really valid.

Democratic rule does not really require a government to respond instantly to public opinion; all that is required is that the public, if dissatisfied, will have an opportunity to change policy sometime in the not-too-distant future. The fact is that all functioning democracies contain some elements that make them less than perfectly responsive to popular opinion; if they did not, they could not operate. Allowing debate to go on endlessly would mean that the government could not reach decisions on most matters. Quiet diplomacy, whether carried out by Henry Kissinger, Paul Warnke, Paul Nitze, or anyone else, is no more "undemocratic" than allowing a U.S. senator to serve for six years before having to stand for election again. At some point, it is necessary to freeze popular opinion and make policy.

Besides, it is mistaken to think that anything like a well-defined "view of the American public" on arms control really exists. As we have seen, three-fourths of the American public can be either for or against arms control, depending on whether the issue being stressed at the moment is limiting arms or verifying compliance. Popular opinion on arms control at any point in time depends greatly on current events and the skill of political leaders in shaping the public debate.

The Congress and the public should be kept informed of current developments in arms control; this makes sense, as they will eventually have to make some judgment on a treaty or on the administration's arms control policy. It is probably also a good idea to keep senators and congressmen informed on the progress of negotiations on an informal basis. But the central issue should not be whether every faction of the American public is represented at Geneva, but whether the policy will be tested by an election at some point.

The ideal American arms control process would look something like this: The administration would articulate the historical problems that traditional forms of arms control—specifically, numerical limits on weapons—have caused. It would explain that, while

198 CALCULATED RISKS

it is not opposed to arms control in principle, in practice arms control is much less important than many policies that the United States can decide entirely on its own, such as strategic weapons policy, levels of defense spending, and military tactics.

The administration would then develop a sensible defense program. The administration would begin by identifying its objectives in its national security policy. It would then define the missions of U.S. armed forces on the basis of these objectives. Finally, it would plan the forces necessary for carrying out these missions—while staying within the limits of a defense budget providing about $240 billion in annual outlays (the high side of the post–World War II historical norm). One of the underlying assumptions of this defense program should be that nuclear weapons are currently suited for little else than deterring a nuclear attack, and that it is possible to provide an effective, survivable deterrent at an affordable cost.

To decide what to do about arms control, the President would appoint an official with near-total authority over U.S. arms control policy; this could be the National Security adviser, but it could also be someone else, so long as he had the solid backing of the President. This arms control "czar" would be expected to consult with experts from the intelligence community (the Director of Central Intelligence or his designee would be appropriate) in order to find out what kinds of agreements could be monitored at acceptable levels of confidence.

The "czar" would also consult with the leaders in the House and the Senate. If the Congress and the bureaucracy insist, they can attend the formal negotiations at Geneva (as they do now)— so long as the real negotiations are being conducted somewhere else. The Senate would have its chance later, during the ratification process, to judge whether the treaty was in the national interest and passed such tests as verifiability. (A smart administration would keep Senate leaders informally posted on arms control progress so the Armed Services, Foreign Relations, and Intelligence Committees could do their homework before the treaty arrived for ratification.)

A good arms control czar would be able to identify agreements that seem feasible, durable, and negotiable. A comprehensive agenda for arms control might look something like this:

- A Hot Line Improvement Agreement, which might include the addition of a video link, a link between the Pentagon and the Soviet General Staff, and perhaps a jointly staffed crisis center.

- A No First Use Treaty—a mutually announced agreement between the Soviet Union and the United States that neither country will initiate the use of nuclear weapons, that neither will initiate nuclear attacks against the other country's cities, and that neither will initiate nuclear attacks against nuclear reactors, dams, or other targets whose destruction would cause substantial, unpredictable collateral damage.

- A Rules of the Road for Space, in which each country would agree not to interfere with the functioning of others' satellites.

- An International Chemical Nonproliferation Treaty, sponsored by the Soviet Union and the United States, in which each signatory country agreed not to develop chemical weapons if it did not currently possess them, and countries currently possessing chemical weapons pledged not to transfer them to other countries. (The United States and the Soviet Union would enforce the treaty as they do the Nuclear Nonproliferation Treaty; defensive equipment, such as gas masks, protective combat dress, and decontamination equipment, would be exempted.)

Unfortunately, the current arms control situation is a perfect negative image of the foregoing scheme. Negotiations are conducted as publicly as one can imagine. (Often the press hears of a proposal before the opposing government does.) In both countries, negotiating positions appear to be hostage to every component or agency of the government. And the arms control agenda is fixed on cutting warheads, cutting launchers, or achieving some other limit that may have little or nothing to do with the likelihood of war or the cost of defense.

The die-hard arms control supporter will probably scoff at the foregoing agreements as insignificant. Yet, their strong point is that they are eminently feasible; there is no reason why they could not all be negotiated within three years. If they were, more progress would have been achieved in arms control than in the preceding forty years, and the risk of wars of mass destruction would be less—not zero, but perhaps as low as is currently possible.

Arms control—informed by an understanding of which agreements work and which are possible—is absolutely essential in the high-tech nuclear age. If weapons cannot be eliminated, then they must be limited; if they cannot be limited, then they must be controlled. The alternative is that they will be used.

NOTES

Chapter One

1. E. J. Dillon, "True Story of the Genesis of the Hague Conference," *Contemporary Review* (1907), pp. 879–882. Also see Calvin De-Armond Davis, *The United States and the Second Hague Conference* (Durham, N.C.: Duke University Press, 1975), pp. 1–5.
2. Davis, pp. 5–10.

Chapter Two

1. U.S. Department of Defense, *Posture Statement for Fiscal Year 1966* (Washington, D.C.: U.S. Government Printing Office, 1966), pp. 211–212; also see the analysis by Ted Greenwood, *The Making of MIRV* (Cambridge, Mass.: Ballinger Publishing Company, 1975), pp. 73–75.
2. See Herbert Stein, *Presidential Economics* (New York: Simon & Schuster, 1984), chap. 5; and William Safire, *Before the Fall* (Garden City, N.Y.: Doubleday & Co., 1975), pp. 509–528.
3. Hector C. Bywater, *Seapower in the Pacific* (London: Constable & Co., 1934), p. 77.
4. See Stephen Roskill, *Naval Policy Between the Wars,* vol. 1 (New York: Walker & Co., 1968).
5. See Bywater, *Seapower in the Pacific.*
6. See John Chalmers Vinson, *The Parchment Peace* (Athens, Ga.: University of Georgia Press, 1955), chaps. 5–9.
7. See Charles Evans Hughes, "Some Aspects of Our Foreign Policy," in *The Pathway to Peace* (New York: Harper & Brothers, 1925), pp. 33–58.

8. Charles Evans Hughes, *The Autobiographical Notes of Charles Evans Hughes*, David J. Danelski and Joseph S. Tulchin, eds. (Cambridge, Mass.: Harvard University Press, 1973), p. 243; italics in original.

9. Harold Sprout and Margaret Sprout, *Toward a New Order of Sea Power* (Princeton, N.J.: Princeton University Press, 1940), pp. 142–143.

10. Yamato Ichihashi, *The Washington Conference and After* (Stanford, Calif.: Stanford University Press, 1928), pp. 7–18.

11. See Sprout and Sprout, pp. 131–134.

12. For example, see the telegram sent by Lord Balfour, the British representative to the conference, to the Foreign Office, No. 60 Telegraphic (A 8763/18/45), November 25, 1921, reprinted as No. 448 in *Documents on British Foreign Policy, 1919–1939*, first series, vol. XIV (London: HMSO) (hereafter *"British Foreign Policy*, first series"). Balfour wrote that the American offer was generous, but he tied the success of the conference to the willingness of the other countries attending to be equally forthcoming.

13. Herbert O. Yardley, *The American Black Chamber*, revised edition (New York: Random House, 1981), pp. 187–211.

14. See Balfour to Curzon, No. 73 Telegraphic (A 8863/18/45), No. 456 in *British Foreign Policy*, first series, vol. XIV; also see Balfour to Curzon No. 185 Telegraphic (A 9501/18/45), No. 513; and Balfour to Curzon No. 191 Telegraphic (A 9567/18/45).

15. United States Senate, *Conference on the Limitation of Armament* (Washington, D.C.: U.S. Government Printing Office, February 10, 1922), p. 867.

16. *Ibid.*, p. 248.

17. *Washington Post*, February 5, 1922; cited also in Ichihashi, p. 348.

18. See *Jane's Fighting Ships* (London: Sampson Low, Marston & Co., 1934), pp. 35–52, 482–488.

19. Hector C. Bywater, *Navies and Nations* (New York: Houghton Mifflin Co., 1927), pp. 48–49.
    In fact, the British themselves seem to have been the originators of the 10,000-ton limit. Royal Naval officials told the British representatives at the conference that such a limit would be in the interest of Britain. See Stephen Roskill, *Naval Policy Between the Wars*, vol. 1 (New York: Walker & Co., 1968), p. 325.

20. Alan Raven and John Roberts, *British Battleships of World War Two* (Annapolis, Md.: Naval Institute Press, 1976), pp. 90–102.

21. *Ibid.*, p. 109.

22. Roskill, *Naval Policy Between the Wars*, vol. 1, p. 332.

23. Raven and Roberts, p. 127.

24. These data were taken from various editions of *Jane's Fighting Ships, Brassey's Naval Annual,* and Raven and Roberts.

    The figure for the costs of the *King George V* is an estimate; no official cost figures seem to exist, other than an estimate for the cost of the armament. In any case, the *King George V* is not essential for this analysis; it was a mongrel design, being designed under the restrictions of arms control, and being modified while under construction in order to take advantage of the breakdown of controls. The real test of the argument is the *Vanguard,* which was designed and built totally free of controls, and for which good cost estimates are available.

Chapter Three

1. See, for example, Arkady Shevchenko's account of talk within the Soviet Ministry of Foreign Affairs in regard to such proposals in *Breaking With Moscow* (New York: Alfred A. Knopf, 1985).

2. For a personal memoir of this period, see Thomas C. Schelling, "What Went Wrong With Arms Control?" *Foreign Affairs* (Winter 1985–86), pp. 219–233. For samples of the product of these seminars, see Hedley Bull, *The Control of the Arms Race* (London: Bradbury Agnew Press, 1961); Thomas C. Schelling and Morton H. Halperin, *Strategy and Arms Control* (New York: The Twentieth Century Fund, 1961); and Donald G. Brennan, ed., *Arms Control, Disarmament, and National Security* (New York: George Braziller, 1961).

3. For a history of the origins of SALT, see John Newhouse, *Cold Dawn: The Story of SALT* (New York: Holt, Rhinehart, & Winston, 1973), pp. 66–102.

4. *Arms Control and Disarmament Agreements,* 1982 edition (Washington, D.C.: Arms Control and Disarmament Agency, 1983), pp. 132–154, 239–277.

5. For Senator Jackson's comments concerning equal limits during the debate in the Senate on SALT I, see U.S. Congress, Senate, *Congressional Record,* 92nd Congress, second session, 1972, vol. 118, no. 130, pp. S13467–13469, and no. 138, pp. S14280–14283. His views were summarized in this passage from his floor speech:

    "The point I wish to make, Mr. President, is that, over the long run, there is no substitute for equal numbers of launchers, taking into account throw-weight differentials. I believe that the Senate should join our negotiators and administration spokesman in rejecting, for the future, the sort of disparities that we have agreed to, on an interim basis, in the present agreement."

6. Bywater, *Navies and Nations,* pp. 162–163.

7. George T. Davis, *A Navy Second to None* (New York: Harcourt, Brace, Jovanovich, 1940), pp. 317–319.
8. Roskill, vol. 1, p. 505.
9. *Ibid.*, p. 500.
10. See the article by Allen Dulles in *Foreign Affairs* (Autumn 1929).
11. Roskill, vol. 1, pp. 112–128.
12. Robert A. Hoover, *Arms Control: The Interwar Naval Limitation Agreements*, Denver Monograph Series in World Affairs, Vol. 17, Book 3 (Denver, Colo.: Graduate School of International Studies, University of Denver, 1980), p. 51; also see Stephen Roskill, *Naval Policy Between the Wars*, vol. 2 (London: Collins, 1976), p. 37.
13. See Introductory Note, Chapter 1, *Documents on British Foreign Policy, 1919–1939*, second series, vol. 1 (London: HMSO) (hereafter *"British Foreign Policy*, second series"), pp. 3–7; Draft Note of Invitation (A 6179/30/45), Document No. 62, *ibid.*, pp. 84–86; and Roskill, vol. 2, pp. 38–48.
14. See *Documents of the London Naval Conference, 1930* (London: HMSO, February 1930). Also see *British Foreign Policy*, second series, pp. 205–311.
15. Thomas A. Beasley, *The Modern History of Japan* (New York: Praeger Publishers, 1963), pp. 236–257; also see Hoover, pp. 47–48.
16. "Notes of Meeting of Representatives of the Delegations of the United States of America, the United Kingdom, and Japan, April 2, 1930," in *British Foreign Policy*, second series, pp. 282–289. In particular, see Appendix II, on p. 288.
17. Hoover, p. 53; Roskill, vol. 2, p. 67.
18. During the SALT I hearings in the Senate, then-Secretary of Defense Melvin Laird said that he would consider the Soviets to be violating the treaty if they deployed any missile that was more than 30 percent larger than the missile that it replaced. See U.S. Senate, Committee on Armed Services, *Military Implications of the Treaty on the Limitation of Anti-Ballistic Missile Systems and the Interim Agreement on Limitation of Strategic Offensive Arms*, 92nd Congress, 2nd Session (Washington, D.C.: U.S. Government Printing Office, 1972).
19. Testimony of Secretary of Defense James R. Schlesinger, U.S. Congress, Senate, Committee on Armed Services, Subcommittee on Arms Control, *Soviet Compliance with Certain Provisions of the 1972 SALT I Agreements*, 94th Congress, 1st Session (Washington, D.C.: U.S. Government Printing Office, 1975).

Chapter Four

1. See Department of Defense, *Soviet Military Power*, 1985 edition (Washington, D.C.: U.S. Government Printing Office, 1985), pp. 25–35.
2. See my "Technological Progress in Strategic Weapons and U.S. Nuclear Policy," *Orbis* (Summer 1985), pp. 241–258.
3. Albert J. Brookes, *Photo Reconnaissance* (London: Ian Allan, Ltd., 1975), p. 10.
4. Joseph E. O'Conner, "Oral History Interview with Robert Amory, Jr." (February 9, 1966), John F. Kennedy Library, pp. 112–117.
5. Jay Miller, *Lockheed U-2* (Austin, Tex.: Aerofax, Inc., 1983), p. 26.
6. A short summary of the development of satellite reconnaissance systems appears in Scott D. Breckinridge, *The CIA and the U.S. Intelligence System* (Boulder, Col.: Westview Press, 1986), pp. 134–143.
7. See U.S. Congress, Senate Committee on Commerce, Science, and Transportation, *NASA Authorization for Fiscal Year 1978*, part 3 (Washington, D.C.: U.S. Government Printing Office, 1977), pp. 1642–1643.
8. "Space Reconnaissance Dwindles," *Aviation Week and Space Technology*, 6 October 1980, pp. 18–20.
9. Department of Defense, *Soviet Military Power*, 1984 edition (Washington, D.C.: U.S. Government Printing Office, 1984), p. 51.
10. *Soviet Military Power*, 1984 edition, pp. 7–8.
11. See Daniel Yankelovich and John Doble, "The Public Mood: Nuclear Weapons and the USSR," *Foreign Affairs* (Fall 1984), pp. 33–46; and *Public Opinion* (August/September 1982), p. 39. A more recent survey with similar results appears in *The Gallup Report* (October 1984), p. 4, which indicated 78 percent of those surveyed favored a "mutual, verifiable freeze."
12. Stephen J. Flanagan, "Managing the Intelligence Community," *International Security* (Summer 1985), p. 79.
13. Fred Charles Iklé, "After Detection, What?" *Foreign Affairs* (January 1961), pp. 208–220.
14. Roskill, *Naval Policy Between the Wars*, vol. 2, p. 371.

Chapter Five

1. See Roskill, *Naval Policy Between the Wars*, vol. 1, p. 309; Ichihashi, pp. 52–53, 354.

2. Ralph E. Lapp, *Atoms and People* (New York: Harper & Brothers, 1956), pp. 102–103.
3. See James Shepley and Clay Blair, Jr., *The Hydrogen Bomb: The Men, The Menace, The Mechanism* (New York: David McKay Co., 1954), p. 115; and Thomas B. Cochran, William M. Arkin, and Milton M. Hoenig, *Nuclear Weapons Databook*, vol. I (Cambridge, Mass.: Ballinger Publishing Co., 1984), pp. 22–26.
4. Herbert F. York, *The Advisors* (San Francisco: W. H. Freeman & Co., 1976), p. 95.
5. Leona Marshall Libby, *The Uranium People* (New York: Crane Russak and Charles Scribner's Sons, 1979), pp. 251–252, 288–293; also see Kosta Tsipis, *Arsenal: Understanding Weapons in the Nuclear Age* (New York: Simon & Schuster, 1983), pp. 35–38; and Cochran, Arkin, and Hoenig, p. 27.
6. Gregg Herken, *The Winning Weapon* (New York: Alfred Knopf, 1980), p. 25.
7. York, p. 20.
8. Shepley and Blair, p. 118.
9. Libby, pp. 290–291.
10. York, p. 29.
11. I. N. Golovin, *I. V. Kurchatov*, 2nd ed. (Moscow: Atomizdat, 1973). Also see the English translation of the first edition by William H. Dougherty (Bloomington, Ind.: Selbstverlag Press, 1968).
12. Golovin, p. 49.
13. *New York Times* (October 4, 1951), p. 6.
14. *Pravda*, October 6, 1951, p. 1.
15. See the article by Harrison Salisbury in *The New York Times*, February 24, 1952, p. 21.
16. Golovin, pp. 66–67.
17. York, pp. 90–91.
18. American sources cited these bombs as having "two and a half times" the yield of the Hiroshima bomb, or about 30 kilotons. See *The New York Times*, September 18, 1953, p. 10.
19. See the story on Soviet weapon designer N. L. Dukhov in *Pravda Ukrainy*, October 26, 1984. Dukhov was originally a tank designer, and was responsible for the JS-III heavy tank that the Soviets used during World War II. He was brought into the Soviet nuclear program in 1948 and, according to the article, the 1949 explosion knocked over one of Dukhov's tanks that had been parked near the test site.
20. Golovin, p. 67.
21. *New York Times*, September 17, 1954, p. 1.

22. S. N. Kozlov *et al., O Sovetskoy Voyennoy Nauke* [On Soviet Military Science] (Moscow: Voyenizdat, 1964), p. 210.

23. *Pravda*, November 28, 1955, p. 1; emphasis added. Also see York, p. 165.

24. From Ralph Lapp, *The Weapons Culture* (New York: W. W. Norton, 1968), p. 100.

25. See Earl H. Voss, *Nuclear Ambush: The Test-Ban Trap* (Chicago: Henry Regnery Co., 1963), p. 57.

Most citations of this proposal have not observed that the recommended test ban would not have gone into effect until the following year. The full text of the Soviet proposal, which was presented at the London Disarmament Conference, is available as United Nations Document DC/SC1/26/Rev. 2, May 10, 1955.

26. See, for example, *Soviet Military Power*, 1985 edition (Washington, D.C.: U.S. Department of Defense, 1985), pp. 58–59, and *Soviet Space Defense Initiatives* (Washington, D.C.: U.S. Department of Defense, 1986).

Chapter Six

1. B. H. Liddell Hart, *The Tanks* (London: Cassell, 1959), pp. 4–5.

2. A. M. Low, *Tanks* (London: Hutchinson & Co., 1941), pp. 12–13.

3. See R. S. Cooper, Director, Defense Advanced Projects Agency, *The U.S. Anti-Satellite Program*, Testimony before Senate Foreign Relations Committee, April 25, 1984 (Washington, D.C.: U.S. Government Printing Office).

4. See *Soviet Military Power*, 1986 edition (Washington, D.C.: U.S. Department of Defense, 1986), pp. 48–52.

5. Bernard Brodie, *The Absolute Weapon* (New York: Harcourt, Brace & Co., 1946), pp. 50–51.

6. See Cochran, Arkin, and Hoenig, *Nuclear Weapons Databook*, vol. I, p. 60.

7. Letter to James Conant, quoted in James Shepley and Clay Blair, Jr. *The Hydrogen Bomb* (New York: David McKay Co., 1954), pp. 59–60.

8. See Kosta Tsipis, "Laser Weapons," *Scientific American* (December 1981), pp. 51–57.

Chapter Seven

1. Harry Wulforst, *Breakthrough to the Computer Age* (New York: Charles Scribner's Sons, 1982), pp. 49–84.

2. Steve J. Heims, *John von Neumann and Norbert Wiener: From Mathematics to the Technologies of Life and Death* (Cambridge, Mass.: MIT Press, 1980), pp. 77–96.

3. John von Neumann and Oskar Morgenstern, *The Theory of Games and Economic Behavior*, 3rd ed. (New York: John Wiley & Sons, 1964).
4. See Fred Kaplan, *The Wizards of Armageddon* (New York: Simon & Schuster, 1983), chapters 2–4.
5. See Bruce L. R. Smith, *The RAND Corporation: Case Study of a Nonprofit Advisory Corporation* (Cambridge, Mass.: Harvard University Press, 1966).
6. See Albert Wohlstetter, "The Delicate Balance of Terror," *Foreign Affairs* (January 1959), pp. 211–234.
7. See Bruce M. Russett, *Prisoners of Insecurity* (San Francisco: W. H. Freeman & Co., 1983), pp. 100–103.
8. See Bywater, *Navies and Nations*, p. 113.
9. Charles Evans Hughes, *Autobiographical Notes*, p. 240. Also see Sprout and Sprout, *Toward a New Order of Sea Power*, pp. 102–114.
10. U.S. Senate Committee on Foreign Relations, *Report of the American Delegation to the Proceedings of the Conference on the Limitation of Armament* (Washington, D.C.: U.S. Government Printing Office, February 3, 1922), p. 18.
11. Curzon to Balfour, No. 66 Telegraphic (A 8863/18/45), *Documents on British Foreign Policy*, second series, pp. 526–527.
12. Barton Whaley, *Covert German Rearmament, 1919–1939: Deception and Misperception* (Frederick, Md.: University Publications of America, 1984), pp. 87–95.
13. See Desmond Ball, "U.S. Strategic Forces: How Would They Be Used?" *International Security* (Winter 1982/1983), pp. 31–60; and Thomas Powers, "Making a Plan for World War III," *The Atlantic* (November 1982), pp. 82–110.
14. See Strobe Talbott, *Deadly Gambits: The Reagan Administration and the Stalemate in Nuclear Arms Control*, 2nd ed. (New York: Vintage Books, 1985), pp. 222–276.

Chapter Eight

1. See my "Intelligence in the Organizational Context: Coordination and Error in U.S. Intelligence Estimates," *Orbis* (Fall 1985), pp. 571–596.
2. "Superpowers Maneuvering for Supremacy on High Seas," *Washington Post* (April 4, 1984), p. A18.2.
3. John Jordan, *Soviet Warships: The Soviet Surface Fleet 1960 to the Present* (Annapolis, Md.: Naval Institute Press, 1984), pp. 10–20.
4. Bruce W. Watson, *Red Navy at Sea: Soviet Naval Operations on*

the High Seas, 1956–1980 (Boulder, Colo.: Westview Press, 1982), p. 183.

5. See Sean M. Lynn-Jones, "A Quiet Success for Arms Control: Preventing Incidents at Sea," *International Security* (Spring 1985), pp. 154–184. Lynn-Jones offers what seems to be the only account of the negotiations leading to the completion of the treaty; his chronology is based on an interview with Herbert Okun, one of the negotiators of the agreement. For this chapter, I used Lynn-Jones's description, along with some conversations with some of the other U.S. participants.

6. For a reprint of the agreement, see *Treaties and Other International Acts, Series 7379* (Washington, D.C.: U.S. Department of State, 1972).

7. S. G. Gorshkov, *Red Star Rising at Sea*, trans. by Theodore A. Neely, Jr. (Annapolis, Md.: U.S. Naval Institute, 1974), pp. 118–119.

8. See Robert P. Hilton, Sr., "The U.S.-Soviet Incidents at Sea Treaty," *Naval Forces* (January 1985), pp. 30–37.

9. For more on this kind of problem, see Graham Allison, *Essence of Decision* (Boston: Little, Brown, 1971).

10. Steven A. Hildreth, *Nuclear Risk Reduction Centers* (Washington, D.C.: Congressional Research Service, November 12, 1986), p. 1.

11. See Sam Nunn and John W. Warner, "Reducing the Risk of Nuclear War," *Washington Quarterly* (Spring 1984), pp. 3–7; also see Richard K. Betts, "A Joint Nuclear Risk Reduction Center," *Parameters* (Spring 1985), pp. 39–51.

12. Richard Nixon, *RN: The Memoirs of Richard Nixon* (New York: Grosset & Dunlap, 1978), pp. 936–942.

13. Jimmy Carter, *Keeping Faith* (New York: Bantam Books, 1982), p. 472.

14. Viktor Suvorov, "GUSM: The Soviet Service of Strategic Deception," *International Defense Review* (August 1985), pp. 1235–1239.

15. "SS-25 Has More Than Double the Throwweight of Predecessor," *Defense Daily* (October 25, 1984), p. 1.

16. *Ibid.*

17. Drew Middleton, "Soviets Said to Deploy a New Missile," *New York Times* (October 22, 1984), p. 3.

Chapter Nine

1. Paul Stares, *The Militarization of Space: U.S. Policy, 1945–84* (Ithaca, N.Y.: Cornell University Press, 1985).

210 *Notes*

2. Stares, pp. 112–117; Herbert F. York, *Race to Oblivion* (New York: Simon & Schuster, 1970), p. 131.
3. Samuel Glasstone and Philip J. Dolan, *The Effects of Nuclear Weapons,* 3rd ed. (Washington, D.C.: Dept. of Defense and Dept. of Energy, 1977), p. 45.
4. Stares, *The Militarization of Space,* pp. 117–120.
5. *Ibid.,* pp. 120–129.
6. Department of Defense, *Soviet Strategic Defense Programs* (Washington, D.C.: U.S. Government Printing Office, 1984), pp. 13, 16.
7. *Ibid.*
8. Office of Technology Assessment, *Anti-Satellite Weapons, Countermeasures, and Arms Control* (Washington, D.C.: U.S. Government Printing Office, 1985), p. 10.
9. Office of Technology Assessment, *Anti-Satellite Weapons,* p. 77.
10. Albert Wohlstetter, "The Delicate Balance of Terror," *Foreign Affairs* (January 1959), pp. 211–234.
11. Bruce Blair, *Strategic Command and Control* (Washington, D.C.: Brookings Institution, 1984).

INDEX

211

Hot Line Agreement (1963),
161–66
critics of, 164–65
Cuban Missile Crisis and, 162,
165
first use of, 164
low-level bureaucracy in, 172
success of, 166, 171, 176
verification of, 167
Hughes, Charles Evans, 32–35,
93, 116, 117, 147–48
Hungary, 12
hydrogen bomb, 59, 95–96, 100,
125
computer program for, 139–40

Iceland Summit (1986), 52, 128
Iklé, Fred, 53, 84
implosion devices, 96, 102
Incidents at Sea Agreement
(1972), 13, 156–61
complaints leading to, 156–57
low-level bureaucracy in, 172
negotiations for, 158–59
practical benefits of, 167
Soviet equality in, 159–60
success of, 160–61, 166, 171,
176
verification of, 167
India, 100, 164, 174
inflation, 25–26, 27
INF (intermediate-range nuclear
forces) talks, 127, 129
intelligence sources, 87–89
on ICBMs, 169–70
SCC and, 168–69
on Soviet missile deployments,
155
Intelsat communications satellite,
161
intercontinental ballistic missile
(ICBM):
intelligence on, 169–70
launch control centers for, 186,
187
launchers for, 74–75
new generation of, 188

scrapped, 93, 94
size of, 70–71, 122
technological asymmetries in,
58–61
throw-weight issue in, 151
vulnerability of, 87–88
intermediate-range ballistic mis-
sile (IRBM), 131–32, 179
Gorbachev 1987 initiative, 128
International Atomic Energy
Agency (IAEA), 173
International Court of Justice, 15
International Peace Conference
(1899), 15
Iran, 73, 174
Iran-Contra arms affair, 128, 129
Iranian Revolution, 27
Ireland, 174
Iron Duke battleship, 41
Israel, 164, 174
Italy, 33–34, 62, 73, 86, 162
Item device, 102, 107
Ivy test series, 103

Jackson, Henry, 60
Japan:
cruisers built by, 38–39
in London Naval Conference,
64–66
in naval arms race, 148, 149
naval power of, 30–31
in Washington Naval Conference agreements, 33–35, 41,
62, 93–94, 146, 147
after World War I, 18
jet engines, 22, 121, 122
Joe 1 test, 105
Johnson, Edwin, 105–6
Johnson, Lyndon B., 54, 164
Joint Atomic Energy Committee,
U.S. Congress, 105–6

Kato, Baron, 34
Kennedy, John F., 23, 112, 179
Keynes, John Maynard, 136
Khrushchev, Nikita, 108, 162,
179

naval power, 29–30
Naval Program (1916), 30, 31,
    147–48
naval treaties, 13
  interwar, 37–38
  see also Washington Naval
    Treaty
Navy, Japanese, 65
Navy, Soviet, 157–60
Navy, U.S., 29–30, 92, 123, 131,
    133, 160–61
Nelson battleship, 35, 43, 45, 46
Netherlands, 30
New Deal, 136
New York Times, 12, 80, 164,
    169
Nicholas II, Czar of Russia, 15,
    54
Nike Zeus antiballistic missile
    system, 179
Nitze, Paul, 74–75
Nixon, Richard M., 25–26, 55, 159
Nixon-Brezhnev summit (1972),
    159
no first use against cities policy,
    193
no first use (NFU) policy, 190–
    193
Nonproliferation Treaty (1968),
    19, 172–76
  Baruch Plan and, 173
  success of, 174–76
  terms of, 174
North Atlantic Treaty Organiza-
    tion (NATO), 123, 126, 127,
    128, 131, 190–92
nuclear energy, 173
nuclear firebreak, 179
nuclear freeze movement, 78–80,
    82
nuclear land mines, 122
nuclear-pumped lasers, 112
nuclear reactors, 173–74
nuclear weapons:
  computers and, 137–41
  cost of, 23–25
  shrinking size of, 121–25

strategic vs. tactical, 125–34
symbolic function of, 171
nuclear weapons tests, 102–3
  in China, 109
  in Soviet Union, 105–11
  in U.S., 102–3
nuclear winter, 193
Nunn, Sam, 163

Office of Technology Assessment
    (OTA), 183–84
oil prices, 26, 27
on-site inspections, 76
Operation Greenhouse, 107
Operation Hardtack II, 111
Operation Ivy, 106
Operation Smokey, 108
operations research and opera-
    tions analysis, 142–43
Oppenheimer, J. Robert, 101, 125
Otto, Nicolaus, 115

Pakistan, 164, 174
Partial Test Ban Treaty (1963),
    18, 111–12, 174
Peacekeeper/MX missile, 70
Permanent Court of Arbitration,
    15–16
Pershing II missile, 127, 128, 132
Philippines, 31, 63
Polaris submarines, 59
Poseidon submarines, 172
Powers, Francis Gary, 73, 178
Powers, Thomas, 123
Pratt, William, 32–33
Pravda, 106
price controls, 25–28
Prisoner's Dilemma game theory,
    144–46
Progressive Era, 31
Pu-239 isotope, 96
public opinion, 78–82
  defense budget and, 84–86
  on nuclear freeze, 79–80, 82
  quiet diplomacy and, 197
  verification issues and, 80–82,
    168

ABOUT THE AUTHOR

BRUCE D. BERKOWITZ, who received his doctorate from the University of Rochester, has held positions in the intelligence community and the United States Congress. Dr. Berkowitz completed this book while in residence as a Visiting Scholar at the Brookings Institution and was previously an International Affairs Fellow of the Council on Foreign Relations. He is the author of *American Security*.